Mohandas Gandhi

These and other titles are included in The Importance Of biography series:

Maya Angelou
Louis Armstrong
James Baldwin
The Beatles
Alexander Graham Bell
Napoleon Bonaparte
Julius Caesar
Rachel Carson
Charlie Chaplin
Charlemagne
Winston Churchill
Christopher Columbus
Leonardo da Vinci
Charles Dickens
Emily Dickinson
Walt Disney
F. Scott Fitzgerald
Anne Frank
Benjamin Franklin
Mohandas Gandhi
Jane Goodall
Martha Graham
Lorraine Hansberry
Stephen Hawking

Ernest Hemingway
Adolf Hitler
Harry Houdini
Thomas Jefferson
John F. Kennedy
Martin Luther King Jr.
Joe Louis
Douglas MacArthur
Thurgood Marshall
Margaret Mead
Golda Meir
Mother Jones
Mother Teresa
John Muir
Richard M. Nixon
Pablo Picasso
Elvis Presley
Eleanor Roosevelt
Margaret Sanger
Oskar Schindler
William Shakespeare
Tecumseh
Pancho Villa
Simon Wiesenthal

Mohandas Gandhi

by Mary and Mike Furbee

Lucent Books, P.O. Box 289011, San Diego, CA 92198-9011

The editor wishes to thank Don Nardo for
his valuable contribution to this book.

Library of Congress Cataloging-in-Publication Data

Furbee, Mary.
   Mohandas Gandhi / by Mary and Mike Furbee.
      p. cm.—(The importance of)
   Includes bibliographical references and index.
   Summary: Discusses the life of Mohandas Gandhi, the
well-known and much revered social reformer and nonviolent protestor, including his childhood and early years,
his work to end discrimination in India, the passive
resistance movement he led, his role in South Africa, and
his legacy.
   ISBN 1-56006-674-1 (lib. bdg. : alk. paper)
   1. Gandhi, Mahatma, 1869–1948. 2. Statesmen—India—
Biography. 3. Nationalists—India—Biography. I. Furbee,
Mike. II. Title. III. Series.
   DS481.G3 F82   2000
   954.03'5'092—dc21   99–050794

Contents

Foreword   7
Important Dates in the Life of
     Mohandas Gandhi   8

INTRODUCTION
The Father of Nonviolence   10

CHAPTER 1
Coming of Age in British India and London   14

CHAPTER 2
From India to the Colonies of South Africa   28

CHAPTER 3
Gandhi's Stormy Return to South Africa   40

CHAPTER 4
The Mahatma Comes Home   55

CHAPTER 5
The Road to Independence   70

CHAPTER 6
Independence at Last   82

EPILOGUE
Gandhi's Legacy   94

Notes   96
Glossary   98
For Further Reading   99
Works Consulted   100
Index   103
Picture Credits   108
About the Authors   108

Foreword

THE IMPORTANCE OF biography series deals with individuals who have made a unique contribution to history. The editors of the series have deliberately chosen to cast a wide net and include people from all fields of endeavor. Individuals from politics, music, art, literature, philosophy, science, sports, and religion are all represented. In addition, the editors did not restrict the series to individuals whose accomplishments have helped change the course of history. Of necessity, this criterion would have eliminated many whose contribution was great, though limited. Charles Darwin, for example, was responsible for radically altering the scientific view of the natural history of the world. His achievements continue to impact the study of science today. Others, such as Chief Joseph of the Nez Percé, played a pivotal role in the history of their own people. While Joseph's influence does not extend much beyond the Nez Percé, his nonviolent resistance to white expansion and his continuing role in protecting his tribe and his homeland remain an inspiration to all.

These biographies are more than factual chronicles. Each volume attempts to emphasize an individual's contributions both in his or her own time and for posterity. For example, the voyages of Christopher Columbus opened the way to European colonization of the New World. Unquestionably, his encounter with the New World brought monumental changes to both Europe and the Americas in his day. Today, however, the broader impact of Columbus's voyages is being critically scrutinized. *Christopher Columbus,* as well as every biography in The Importance Of series, includes and evaluates the most recent scholarship available on each subject.

Each author includes a wide variety of primary and secondary source quotations to document and substantiate his or her work. All quotes are footnoted to show readers exactly how and where biographers derive their information, as well as provide stepping stones to further research. These quotations enliven the text by giving readers eyewitness views of the life and times of each individual covered in The Importance Of series.

Finally, each volume is enhanced by photographs, bibliographies, chronologies, and comprehensive indexes. For both the casual reader and the student engaged in research, The Importance Of biographies will be a fascinating adventure into the lives of people who have helped shape humanity's past and present, and who will continue to shape its future.

IMPORTANT DATES IN THE LIFE OF MOHANDAS GANDHI

1757
The East India Company, a powerful English trading firm established by Queen Elizabeth I in 1600, succeeds over other imperial powers and lays claim to India.

1888
Gandhi leaves India to attend law school in London, England.

1869
Mohandas K. Gandhi is born in Porbandar in western India.

1906
Gandhi, now thirty-seven, speaks at a mass meeting in Johannesburg on September 11. He launches a campaign of nonviolent resistance (satyagraha) to protest discrimination against Indians.

| 1757 | 1857–1858 | 1869 | 1883 | 1888 | 1893 | 1906 | 1913 |

1857–1858
Indian soldiers launch a failed rebellion against the East India Company. The British government dissolves the company and takes direct control of India.

1883
Gandhi marries at age thirteen.

1913
Gandhi steps up the intensity of satyagraha. Thousands of South African Indians are jailed.

1893
Gandhi leaves for Johannesburg, South Africa, to work as a lawyer for a group of Muslim businessmen and is thrown out of a first-class train car because he is "colored."

1918
Gandhi is imprisoned for the first time. He writes the pamphlet *Hind Swaraj (Indian Home Rule)*.

1916
Gandhi travels to Champaran to investigate complaints of British mistreatment of indigo farmers.

1930
Gandhi leads a 165-mile march to the Gujarat coast of the Arabian Sea and violates the salt laws. The march is a gesture of defiance against the British monopoly in salt production.

1948
Partitioning of Pakistan and India begins. Violence erupts between Muslims and Hindus. Gandhi begins a fast unto death unless India pledges to stop the violence; a Hindu extremist assassinates Gandhi because of his tolerance for Muslims.

1914	1916	1919	1930	1932	1946	1947	1948

1914
The most discriminatory of South African laws, the Asiatic Registration Law (or Black Act), is repealed. Mohandas Gandhi returns to India at age forty-five, after spending over twenty years in South Africa. The name Mahatma ("Great Soul") is given to him by the famous Indian poet Tagore.

1919
An antisedition act spurs Gandhi to lead nonviolent protests and resistance. In Amritsar, British troops fire on an unarmed crowd, killing 379 Indians.

1932
Mahatma Gandhi begins a "fast unto death" to protest the treatment of India's untouchables.

1947
India becomes free after two hundred years of British rule.

1946
Britain begins the process of leaving India. The prospect that India will be divided into India and Pakistan becomes likely. Gandhi fights the partition.

The Father of Nonviolence

The Indian social reformer Mohandas K. Gandhi was one of the most renowned, controversial, and influential world leaders of the twentieth century. After devoting some twenty years of his life to achieving civil rights for Indians living in South Africa, he went on to lead the movement to free India from British colonial rule. These were unusually ambitious, humanitarian goals and deeds to be sure; but what was most remarkable about them were the methods by which they were implemented. Gandhi consistently used nonviolent protest as a means of bringing about social and political change. And in so doing, he proved to the world that a large-scale revolutionary movement could, contrary to the common wisdom of the time, be waged nonviolently. For this reason, he is widely and deservedly remembered as the "father" of nonviolent political activism.

SATYAGRAHA

Gandhi's peace-loving philosophy developed over the course of several years as a reaction to the widespread violence, racial and religious intolerance, and social divisions and injustices he witnessed in South Africa and India during the late 1800s and early 1900s. To combat and hopefully eradicate these problems, he came to advocate a method of nonviolent resistance that he called satyagraha, loosely translated into English as "the force of truth and love." (In his native language of Gujarati, the word *satya* means "truth and love" and *graha* means "firmness.") Instrumental in developing the concept was Gandhi's reading of the essay "Civil Disobedience," composed by the nineteenth-century American writer and social philosopher Henry David Thoreau. In the essay, Thoreau explains that he had refused to pay his poll tax and willingly went to jail as a way of protesting his government's prosecution of the Mexican-American War, which he viewed as an immoral enterprise. In 1922 Gandhi defined and explained his own brand of civil protest, satyagraha, this way:

> The term . . . was coined by me in South Africa to express the force that the Indians there used for full eight years, and it was coined in order to distinguish it from the movement then going on in the United Kingdom and South Africa under the name of

Passive Resistance. . . . Satyagraha differs from Passive Resistance as the North Pole from the South. The latter has been conceived as a weapon of the weak and does not exclude the use of physical force or violence for the purpose of gaining one's end, whereas the former [satyagraha] has been conceived as a weapon of the strongest and excludes the use of violence in any shape or form. . . . Satyagraha largely appears to the public as Civil Disobedience or Civil Resistance. . . . There come occasions, generally rare, when [the civil resister] considers certain laws to be so unjust as to render obedience to them a dishonor. He then openly and civilly breaks them and quietly suffers the penalty for their breach.[1]

According to the theory, if enough people protested in this way, the government would be forced to listen to them and would seriously consider changing unjust laws or policies.

INEVITABLE SUFFERING

But theory is one thing and practice is often quite another. The question Gandhi had to answer for himself was whether, in the cold light of the social and political realities of his day, such nonviolent resistance could actually bring about social change. In some people's minds, there was the real chance that civil resistance would fail to move or force a government to institute change. More likely, the au-

thorities would react only by beating, arresting, and/or jailing the protesters. Indeed, Gandhi fully realized that satyagraha would demand great sacrifices from its practitioners. He himself willingly submitted to imprisonment on many occasions and taught his followers to do the same. Unfortunately, suffering

Mohandas Gandhi, the "father" of nonviolent political activism. Gandhi used his brand of nonviolent protest, satyagraha, to win India's independence from Great Britain in 1947.

THOREAU'S INFLUENCE ON GANDHI

Gandhi was strongly influenced by the writings of American poet Henry David Thoreau (1817–1862). Thoreau believed, like Gandhi, that God dwells in the soul of the individual. In 1849 Thoreau wrote his essay "Civil Disobedience," which advocated refusing to obey unjust laws. It is the duty of each individual, he said, to determine right from wrong and then obey his or her conscience.

"Unjust laws exist; shall we be content to obey them, or shall we endeavor to amend them . . . or shall we transgress them at once? Men generally, under such a government as this, think that they ought to wait until they have persuaded the majority to alter them. They think that, if they should resist, the remedy would be worse than the evil. But it is the fault of the government itself that the remedy *is* worse than the evil. . . . If the injustice is part of the necessary friction of the machine of government, let it go, let it go; perchance it will wear smooth—certainly the machine will wear out. If the injustice has a spring, or a pulley, or a rope, or a crank, exclusively for itself, then perhaps you may consider whether the remedy will not be worse than the evil; but if it is of such a nature that it requires you to be the agent of injustice to another, then, I say, break the law. Let your life be a counter friction to stop the machine."

Nineteenth-century American writer Henry David Thoreau.

of one kind or another was an inevitable part of civil resistance, he told them; but it would not be in vain, for their suffering would surely focus attention on unjust laws and customs and thereby force those in power to change the system. "Non-violence in its dynamic condition means conscious suffering," he wrote in 1942.

It does not mean meek submission to the will of the evil-doer, but it means the pitting of one's whole soul against the will of the tyrant. Working under this law of our being, it is possible for a single individual to defy the whole might of an unjust empire to save his honor, his religion, his soul, and lay the foundation for that empire's fall or its regeneration.[2]

Incredibly, or so it seemed to many people around the world at the time, Gandhi's nonviolent strategy worked time and again. In both South Africa and India, he and his followers suc-ceeded in changing government policy; and their efforts set in motion the process that resulted in India gaining its independence from Britain. In addition, Gandhi's employment of civil resistance forced governments and entire societies to reexamine and question their traditional moral standards. This was because his philosophy and methods invariably appealed to the human conscience, demanding fair treatment and justice for all. This was the basis for U.S. secretary of state George C. Marshall's famous remark (made in 1948) that Gandhi was "the spokesman for the conscience of mankind."[3]

Chapter

1 Coming of Age in British India and London

Mohandas Karamchand Gandhi was born on October 2, 1869, in the town of Porbandar, located in western India near the coast of the Arabian Sea. (He would not receive his more familiar nickname of Mahatma, meaning "Great Soul," until he was an adult.) Mohandas's father, Karamchand, and his mother, Putlibai (Karamchand's fourth wife; the other three had all died), had four children. Mohandas, who was called Mohan, was the youngest of the four children. He was seven years old when Karamchand Gandhi moved his family 120 miles inland to the larger city of Rajkot in 1876.

The elder Gandhi, who had served as a civil servant in Porbandar, had accepted the prestigious post of *diwan*, or prime minister, of Rajkot, which was a small state as well as a city. At the time, Rajkot was one of hundreds of mostly tiny Indian princedoms that were not subject to direct British rule. At least this was the official situation. In reality, the vast majority of independent Indian princes were British puppets who collaborated with British leaders in return for favors, such as the protection of the British army and lucrative trade deals with the wealthy British Empire. In all, these in-

dependent states encompassed about 40 percent of India's territory and roughly a quarter of its population.

The rest of India's more than 200 million people had been under direct British control since 1858. Although British rule was not tyrannical per se, most British, who were Christians, felt that they were culturally and spiritually superior to the Indians, who were mostly Hindus and Muslims (making up some 70 and 25 percent of the population respectively). Years later, a grown-up Mohandas Gandhi recalled some of the cruel, insensitive treatment Indians endured as a result of this British sense of superiority:

> In those days Christian missionaries used to stand in a corner near the high school and hold forth [preach], pouring abuse on Hindus and their gods. I could not endure this. . . . About the same time, I heard of a well known Hindu having been converted to Christianity. It was the talk of the town that, when he was baptized, he had to eat beef and drink liquor, and that he also had to change his clothes [to European dress]. . . . I also heard that the new convert had already be-

How Britain Viewed India

In 1857 Atlantic Monthly *magazine ran the article "British India," excerpted here. The article presented the two dominant attitudes of Britain and other Western nations toward India at the time. First, India lacked unity, which made it easy to conquer. Second, the Indians were morally and intellectually inferior to white Westerners and were therefore deserving of conquest.*

"We are so accustomed to speak of India as if it constituted one country, and were inhabited by homogeneous people . . . [but] not even in Europe are nations to be found more unlike to one another than in British India. . . . [Indians] differ in moral, physical, and intellectual conditions—in modes of thought and in modes of life. This is one of the chief causes of England's supremacy, just as a similar state of things . . . promoted the conquests of Rome. . . . The peculiar condition of India a hundred years since enabled the English to lay the foundations of their power in that country so broadly and so deep that nothing short of a moral convulsion can uproot them."

Mohandas Gandhi grew up experiencing British prejudice toward Indians.

gun abusing the religion of his ancestors, their customs and their country.[4]

Such religious bigotry was only the tip of the iceberg, so to speak. The British also imposed their laws, court system, language, educational institutions, and social customs on the Indians. All across India, no native Indian could hope to be successful in business or politics unless he adopted at least

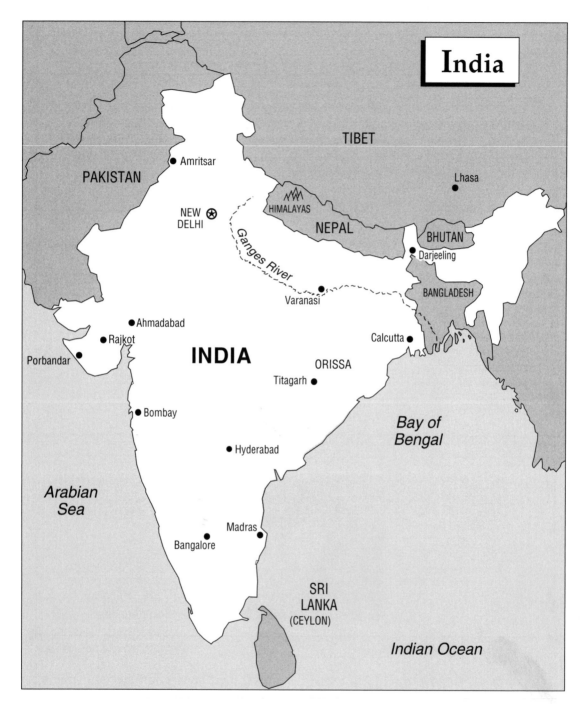

India

TIBET

PAKISTAN

Amritsar

Lhasa

NEW
DELHI ⊗

HIMALAYAS

NEPAL

BHUTAN

Ganges River

Darjeeling

BANGLADESH

Varanasi

Ahmadabad

Calcutta

Rajkot

INDIA

ORISSA

Porbandar

Titagarh

Bombay

Bay of
Bengal

Hyderabad

Arabian
Sea

Madras

Bangalore

SRI
LANKA
(CEYLON)

Indian Ocean

some of the outward trappings of British culture. Thus, even though they lived outside of British-controlled territory, Karam-chand Gandhi and his family felt the effects of British rule and anti-Indian prejudice. Like other Indians, Karamchand knew that

India would never become a strong, independent country, proud of its ancient beliefs and customs, as long as the land remained under Britain's thumb. But during his tenure as *diwan* of Rajkot and throughout the years of his son Mohandas's childhood, few Indians believed that an independent India was anything more than a pipe dream.

A HARDWORKING FATHER AND SPIRITUAL MOTHER

Young Mohandas certainly did not show much if any interest in politics and concentrated his attention instead, as other Indian children did, on his family life and schoolwork. His parents' home was a relatively modest one. This might seem unusual considering that his father held a high position in local government; however, the very fact that Karamchand Gandhi had risen to such high political office was in itself unusual. This was because the Gandhis belonged to the Vaisya, or merchant caste, while civil servants most often came from the higher, more prestigious Kshatriya caste. Castes were rigidly set social classes. Children inherited their caste, or fixed social standing, from their parents. Because certain occupations were reserved for specific castes, children often knew from an early age not only what their lifelong social status would be but also what they would do for a living. Brahmans, the highest caste, were priests; Kshatriyas made up the nobility; the Vaisyas were small farmers and merchants; the Sudras were peasants and laborers; and beneath them all were the lowly untouchables, who were only allowed to work at the least desirable jobs, such as cleaning toilets. Because civil servants were in short supply in Rajkot and neighboring princedoms, and also because the men of the Gandhi family had reputations as excellent managers and shrewd negotiators, Mohandas's grandfather and father had been able to move from merchant status to the higher civil servant status, despite their belonging to a lower caste.

But though Karamchand Gandhi was a dedicated public servant, hard worker, and made more money than most men in his caste, his family remained of modest means. He was not interested in becoming wealthy and held fast to Hindu beliefs that required him to spend his extra income on charity rather than on his own family. Karamchand even planned to leave his children almost no inheritance. Still, the Gandhi home was comfortable, and Mohandas, the pampered baby of the family, had a large, airy room to himself. He even had his own nanny, a kind older woman named Rambha.

Though Mohandas respected his father, he was a good deal closer to his mother, partly because he admired her deep religious faith. His own later intense sense of spirituality was undoubtedly in many ways shaped by her devotion to her Hindu faith and the many ways she practiced its beliefs in her everyday life. "She would not think of taking her meals without her daily prayers," he later wrote.

As far as my memory can go back, I do not remember her having ever missed the Chaturmas [a four-month-long religious fast, similar in many ways to the Christian Lent]. She would take the hardest vows and keep them without flinching. Illness was no excuse for relaxing them. . . . To keep two or three consecutive fasts was nothing to her. Living on one meal a day during Chaturmas was a habit with her. . . . During [one] Chaturmas she vowed not to have food without seeing the sun. We children on those days would stand, staring at the sky, waiting to announce the appearance of the sun to our mother. And I remember days when, at his sudden appearance, we would rush to announce it to her. She would run out to see with her own eyes, but by that time the fugitive sun would be gone [behind some clouds], thus depriving her of her meal. "That does not matter," she would say cheerfully, "God did not want me to eat today." And then she would return to her round of [household] duties.[5]

Putlibai Gandhi set a spiritual example for her children in other ways as well. She often invited traveling monks to recite verses from sacred Hindu books, for example. And every day she faithfully attended temple service. In addition, Putlibai helped anyone who was sick or needy, and unlike the wives of other merchants and civil servants, she did not wear jewels or silk saris. She thought that spending money on showy luxury items was wasteful and showed a lack of humility. People's actions, she taught Mohandas, meant far more than their professed beliefs.

Still another spiritual life lesson that Mohandas learned from his mother was to have tolerance and respect for religious beliefs that differed from his own. Putlibai herself followed the religious customs and practices of several different Hindu sects, something most Hindus did not do. The pursuit of truth, regardless of its source, she said, was more important than blind belief. There might be shreds of truth in all religions, therefore, even in Christianity. This was difficult for the boy to grasp at first, considering the insensitive and often mean-spirited manners displayed by most of the Christians he had seen. But in time he would come to see that his mother was right.

Putlibai Gandhi also taught her son Mohandas the most severe form of Hindu vegetarianism and fasting, eating habits and customs that would eventually come to have a profound effect on his life. The Gandhis were strictly vegetarian because they believed it was morally wrong to take an animal's life. Putlibai took this philosophy even further and did not eat vegetables that grew underground because of the "violence" done to them when they were pulled out of the soil.

LESSONS IN SCHOOL AND LIFE

Although young Mohandas's home life was generally stable and pleasant, his early school days were difficult. At home, the Gandhis spoke Gujarati, one of the dozens of languages spoken in In-

An 1886 photo shows Gandhi (right) with his brother Laxmidas. Gandhi was the youngest of four children.

dia. However, the school he attended was run by the British; thus, Mohandas had to learn some basic English before he could learn anything else. Added to this difficulty was the fact that outside of his home the boy was painfully shy. "I avoided all company," he later recalled.

My books and my lessons were my sole companions. To be at school at the stroke of the hour and to run back home as soon as the school closed,— that was my daily habit. I literally ran back, because I could not bear to talk to anybody. I was even afraid lest anyone should poke fun at me.[6]

Historians have searched in vain for some early signs of greatness in the young Mohandas Gandhi, and he himself later admitted that he was for the most part quite an unremarkable child. About these early years he later wrote, "My memory must have been sluggish and my intellect raw. . . . There is hardly anything to note about my studies. I could only have been a mediocre student."[7] On the other hand, the boy did display some qualities that hinted at the man he would become. He absolutely refused to cheat, for instance. He also took his responsibilities very seriously and was fanatically punctual. Each day, he timed his daily walk to school with great care, insistent on arriving on time. He even sometimes skipped breakfast to make sure he would not be late.

When Mohandas was twelve, he finished elementary school and began attending Rajkot's local secondary school, Alfred Boy's High School. There, he finally began to overcome his shyness, managing to make a few friends with whom he played ball in the streets. Because he was small and insecure, Mohandas looked up to more daring, stronger boys, which sometimes led him into mischief. One friend in particular, a Muslim boy named Sheik Mehtab, briefly led him astray, convincing him to smoke cigarettes and much worse—to steal some gold pieces from one of the older Gandhi brothers. Soon afterward, wracked with guilt, Mohandas wrote a letter to his father admitting the theft and promising never to steal again. "I had thought that he'd be angry, say hard things, and strike his forehead," Mohandas later remembered. Instead, to the boy's surprise, Karamchand Gandhi quietly cried, tore up the letter, and said nothing. The boy knew that his father had forgiven him

and learned an important life lesson from the incident. "A clean confession," the adult Mohandas would say, "combined with a promise never to commit the sin again, when offered before one who has the right to receive it, is the purest type of repentence."[8]

It was during his friendship with Sheik Mehtab that young Mohandas first questioned one of the underpinnings of his faith—vegetarianism. Sheik, a strongly built boy, told him that the Muslims and the British drew their strength from eating meat, adding that the Hindus would always be weak and dependent because they unwisely refrained from consuming meat. Although he feared his parents' reaction if they found out, Mohandas decided to sample some meat dishes. Later, the boy felt so guilty that he confessed his sin to his parents; and once more he felt the cleansing power of their love and forgiveness. In awe of that power, Mohandas vowed never to eat meat again and also to always be as forgiving to others as his parents had been to him.

MARRIAGE AT AN EARLY AGE

Mohandas's rocky experiences at school and with friends soon proved to be only the beginning of a series of new growing pains and life lessons. In 1883, when he was just thirteen, the boy was obliged to marry a girl named Kasturbai, who was also only thirteen. In keeping with ancient Hindu tradition, Mohandas's and Kasturbai's parents had arranged the match back when the two were seven years old.

But Mohandas had not really understood what this betrothal meant at the time; the moment he actually grasped that he was to be married was when the tailor came to measure him for his wedding suit. The boy was at least relieved to learn that, for the foreseeable future, he did not need to make a lot of money to support his new wife. After the ceremony, Kasturbai and Mohandas lived in his parents' house, which meant they did not need separate housing, property, income, or household furnishings.

As a young, immature husband, Mohandas was authoritarian, possessive, petty, and jealous. He demanded that "Ba," as he called Kasturbai, ask permission to go out and play; and then when she did ask, he said "no" just to exert his authority. Yet Kasturbai did not always take this kind of bullying meekly, for the two fought and sometimes did not speak for days, which was stressful for both of them. Years later the adult Mohandas Gandhi would say that he learned about noncooperation (the basis for civil resistance) from his wife. The more tyrannical he was, in fact, the more she refused to cooperate and disobeyed. "It is from Ba that I have learnt passive resistance," he would write many years later, after her death. "She was my better half."[9]

The irritation and emotional stress Mohandas felt during the disagreements with his young wife soon paled into insignificance beside his first experiences with real emotional pain. In 1885, when he was sixteen, his father died after a long illness; and shortly afterward, Kasturbai gave birth to a baby boy, who only lived a few days. Sad-dened, Mohandas grieved for his father, whom he had respected a great deal. As for his firstborn's premature death, the young man believed that this was God's way of saying that children should not marry so young; for the rest of his life, he voiced his disapproval of this tradition, which he had been forced to follow.

FROM HIGH SCHOOL TO LAW SCHOOL

Not surprisingly, Mohandas's stress over his marital problems and his grief over the death of his father and son caused his schoolwork to suffer for a while. But he eventually managed to pull himself together and finished high school with respectable grades. Toward the end he even began to enjoy mathematics and geometry, which had once been his least favorite subjects. Also making his spirits brighten was the fact that Kasturbai had another baby about the time of his school graduation in 1888. This one, a boy whom they named Harilal, thankfully survived infancy.

Having graduated from school, Mohandas faced a tough decision. Should he settle down for good in Rajkot, or should he go on to higher education in an effort to better himself? A family friend suggested that he study law in England. This would not only prepare him to follow in his father's footsteps as a high-ranking local public official, but it would also give him the prestige of having a British college degree, something only a few Indians possessed. There was no telling what opportunities might materialize for a young Indian man with such credentials. His head filled with these thoughts, Mohandas was excited about the prospect of studying abroad and hurried to tell his mother of his decision.

To his dismay, however, Putlibai Gandhi was firmly opposed to his leaving India. She told him that she considered England a corrupt land where people had loose morals. Only when her son vowed in front of a priest not to touch meat, alcohol, or

Gandhi and his wife Kasturbai. The couple was married when they were only thirteen years old.

women while abroad did she relent and give him her blessings. The elders of their caste, however, were not to be persuaded. They called Mohandas to meet with them and told him they were adamantly opposed to his plans. "Your proposal to go to England is not proper," exclaimed the leading elder. "Our religion forbids voyages abroad. We have also heard that it is not possible to live there without compromising our religion. One is obliged to eat and drink with Europeans!" Mohandas remained firm, however, boldly telling the elders, "I think the caste should not interfere in the matter."[10] The price of this defiance was his expulsion from the caste. This strong vote of disapproval and censure affected his family, for it meant that other caste members were forbidden to visit with them, marry into their family, or lend them money. Yet Mohandas's relatives stood by him and told him he should make his own decisions regardless of what the "old-fashioned" elders said and did.

A young Mohandas Gandhi in Western dress. Overwhelmed by cultural differences, Gandhi found it difficult to adjust to life in London.

ADJUSTING TO ENGLISH LIFE

Mohandas Gandhi was therefore filled with confidence when he sailed for England on September 4, 1888, although he did regret leaving Kasturbai and the infant Harilal behind. When he reached London eight weeks later, the young man was eager to begin studying law. He enrolled at a small but prestigious law school called the Inner Temple. Realizing that a firm grasp of English was necessary for one to succeed in such a school and that his command of English was still not complete, he began reading daily newspapers for practice. The *Daily News*, *Daily Telegraph*, and *Pall Mall Gazette* became his constant companions during the initial months of his law studies.

During these first months in London, Gandhi also tried diligently to adjust to English life, a task he found very difficult due to the marked differences between the cultures of England and his native India. In particular, he had a hard time at first finding the foods he needed to stick to his vegetarian diet. Most of the university students in London ate many meals in restaurants, where the fare was based almost entirely on meat. And at the small boardinghouse where he found lodgings, his landlady had never met a vegetarian before; a well-meaning woman, she tried to fill him up with bread and oatmeal. But both his Indian and English friends told Gandhi that he would not survive the northern climate on bread and oatmeal alone. Many Hindus he met had begun eating meat, and Gandhi soon became embarrassed that he was not abandoning his "backward" Indian ways, too. Nevertheless, he remained a vegetarian, mainly because, after many weeks of searching, he was fortunate enough to discover two vegetarian restaurants that served balanced and tasty meatless meals.

Finding these vegetarian outlets also opened up a new and very much needed social life for Gandhi. He found that there was an organization called the London Vegetarian Society, joined it, and met numerous new friends whose eating habits were similar to his own. In fact, he felt much more comfortable in the company of vegetarians than with any other people he met in England.

Many of his new friends were intellectuals who were rethinking social and political traditions and systems. Through them, he was introduced to the works of important Western writers such as English poet Percy Bysshe Shelley, American poet Henry David Thoreau, and Russian novelist Leo Tolstoy. These authors sought to reexamine commonly held beliefs about religion, government, and human rela-

tionships. Constantly exposed to new and stimulating ideas, Gandhi thrived.

GANDHI REDISCOVERS HINDUISM

Gandhi's experiences with his vegetarian friends also expanded his knowledge and appreciation of his own Hindu faith. At meetings of the vegetarian society, Gandhi met Englishmen who were studying the Hindu religion. At first these men were shocked that, despite his having been raised a Hindu, Gandhi had never read the *Bhagavad Gita*, a lengthy epic poem that constitutes almost a sacred text to Hindus. They gave him an English translation of the poem by English scholar and poet Sir Edwin Arnold. Gandhi found it eye-opening that some Westerners believed Hinduism was worthy of study.

From the day Gandhi opened the *Bhagavad Gita*, he became, for the first time in his life, a serious student of the Hindu religion. He was particularly struck by the themes of pacifism and eternal life developed in the poem. As the story unfolds, the hero, Arjuna, goes to war against his enemies, but finding that many of them are related to him by blood, he lays down his weapons and vows not to fight. Then the god Vishnu, taking the physical form of the charioteer Krishna, commands Arjuna to do his duty no matter how difficult. Vishnu tells him that the human soul is part of the universal soul, so his relatives do not really die but will live on in the spiritual sense.

Gandhi's interest in religion caught fire. After reading the Hindu texts, he moved on

THE *BHAGAVAD GITA*

The Hindu religious text known as the Bhagavad Gita, *which greatly influenced Gandhi, was written between the third and fourth centuries* A.D. *An epic poem, it tells the story of the hero Arjuna, who goes to war against his enemies and in the process meets the god Vishnu, who has taken human form. This excerpt from the work illustrates one of its central concepts—that God dwells in everything.*

"I am taste in water, son of Kunti,
I am light in the moon and sun.
The sacred syllable Om of all the Vedas,
Sound in ether, manliness in men.
I am the goodly odor in earth,
And brilliance in fire am I,
Life in all beings,
And austerity in ascetics am I.
Know me as the eternal seed of all beings.
I am intelligence of the intelligent.
Majesty of the majestic am I.
I am the soul, Gudakesa,
that abides in the heart of all beings."

An ornate image of the god Vishnu from a thirteenth-century Hindu temple.

INDIAN ATTITUDES ABOUT BRITISH RULE

In the 1871 article "British Rule," excerpted from Indian writer Dadabhai Naoroji's Essays, Speeches, Addresses, and Writings, *Naoroji sums up commonly held Indian ideas about the pros and cons of foreign rule, which would later become part of the focus of Gandhi's political efforts.*

"The Benefits of British Rule: In the cause of humanity, abolition of suttee [the ancient custom of killing widows when their husbands died] and infanticide . . . allowing remarriage of Hindu widows, and charitable aid in time of famine. . . . In the cause of civilization, education, both male and female. . . . Politically, peace and order, freedom of speech and liberty of the press. . . . Materially, loans for railways and irrigation, development of . . . exports. . . . No nation on the face of the earth has ever had the opportunity of achieving such a glorious work. The Detriments of British Rule: Politically, repeated breach of pledges to give the natives a fair and reasonable share in the higher administration of their own country, which has much shaken confidence in the good faith of the British word. . . . Financially, new modes of taxation, without any adequate effort to increase the means of the people to pay, and . . . inequitable financial relations between England and India. . . . Materially, the continuous impoverishment and exhaustion of the country . . . the great mass of the poor [having] hardly tuppence [two British pennies] a day and a few rags, or a scanty subsistence."

to the sacred texts of other faiths. Among his favorites was Jesus' Sermon on the Mount, which appears in the Book of Matthew in the New Testament. It "went straight to my heart," he later recalled.

I compared it with the [*Bhagavad*] *Gita*. The verses, "But I say unto you, that ye resist not evil; but whosoever shall smite thee on thy right cheek, turn to him the other also. And if any man take away thy coat, let him have thy cloak too," delighted me beyond measure. . . . My young mind tried to unify the teaching of the *Gita* . . . and the Sermon on the Mount. That renunciation [refusal to react to violence with more violence] was the highest form of religion appealed to me greatly.[11]

In addition to reading the daily newspapers and immersing himself in the ins and outs of vegetarianism and religion, Gandhi of course tackled his law studies. Given his many outside interests, it is fortunate that he found the study of law to be reasonably easy, requiring little actual studying. Citing the academic requirements, he later recalled,

> There were two conditions which had to be fulfilled before a student was formally called to the bar: "keeping terms," for twelve terms—equivalent to about three years of study; and passing examinations. Keeping terms . . . meant attending at least six out of about twenty-four dinners in a term. . . . I could not see then, nor have I seen since, how these dinners qualified the students better for the bar. . . . The curriculum of study was easy, barristers [lawyers] being humorously known as "dinner barristers." Everyone knew that the examination had practically no value. In my time there were two, one in Roman Law and the other in Common Law. There were regular textbooks prescribed for these examinations which could be taken in compartments, but scarcely any one read them. . . . Question papers were easy and examiners were generous. The percentage of passes in the Roman Law examination used to be 95 to 99 and of those in the final examination 75 or even more.[12]

On June 10, 1891, Gandhi passed his examinations and was called to the bar. He had learned much in his three years in London. First, he had learned how to live independently; second, he had come to admire much about the British; and third, he had come to value his Hindu heritage more than he had when he was growing up in India. However, in London he had been exposed only to a small, freethinking, fair-minded social circle, and had not learned much about the nature of English colonialism or about the Indian law that he was supposed to begin practicing. He would soon experience a rude awakening to the real world, which he would find not nearly so freethinking and fair-minded.

2 From India to the Colonies of South Africa

In 1891 Gandhi returned to India to find that his mother had died. His family had not told him for fear he might have abandoned his studies before finishing them, thereby jeopardizing his future. He later described the bad news as a "severe shock" and his grief as "even greater than over my father's death. Most of my cherished hopes were shattered. But I remember that I did not give myself up to any wild expression of grief. I could even check the tears, and took to life just as though nothing had happened."[13]

Though he managed to take his mother's death in stride, Gandhi found that readjusting to life in India was difficult. After his experiences in London, his hometown of Rajkot seemed a small and unimportant place. He also found it impossible to make a living as a lawyer because he knew little about Indian law and was therefore unable to attract any clients. Moreover, some members of his caste refused to hire him because they were still angry with him for leaving India in the first place.

Thus, it quickly became clear to Gandhi that he sorely needed further legal training. Leaving his wife and son in Rajkot, he moved to the large Indian city of Bombay to study Indian law and to try his first

cases. His family still expected great things of him; but unfortunately, during his first case he was so miserably shy that he could barely speak. He later described the experience this way:

> I had serious misgivings as to whether I should be able to earn even a living by the profession. About this time I took up the case of one Mamibai. It was a very small case. . . . This was my debut in . . . court. I appeared for the defendant and had thus to cross-examine the plaintiff's witnesses. I stood to speak but my heart sank into my boots. My head was reeling and I felt as though the whole court was doing likewise. I could think of no question to ask. The judge must have laughed and the other lawyers no doubt enjoyed the spectacle. But I was past seeing anything. I sat down and told the [judge] I could not conduct the case, and that he had better engage [another lawyer].[14]

Soon afterward, Gandhi returned to Rajkot feeling defeated. He still lacked confidence, experience, and familiarity with Indian law, so he could expect to earn little money. To make matters worse, one of his older brothers had spent much of the family's money, running it deeply into debt, yet expected Gandhi to pay the bills. "My elder brother," Gandhi later wrote,

assumed that I should have a swinging practice and had, in that expectation, allowed the household expenses to become top-heavy. . . . New things were added every day. . . . How was the [way out of the mess] to be found? To start practice in Rajkot would have meant sure ridicule. I had hardly the knowledge of a [simple law clerk] and yet I expected to be paid ten times his fee! No client would be fool enough to engage me. And even if such a one was to be found, should I add arrogance and fraud to my ignorance and increase my debt to the world?[15]

A SOUTH AFRICAN HAILS GANDHI BEFORE APARTHEID'S ABOLITION

Perhaps more than any other leader in the twentieth century, Gandhi influenced movements for independence and equal rights. In 1970, during the struggle against South African apartheid (the local system of enforced white supremacy), Andre Brink, a noted South African novelist and professor, hailed Gandhi as a great influence during one of his lectures. This excerpt from his lecture is taken from the African National Congress website.

"I feel very proud and very humble to have the privilege of delivering this Memorial Lecture just one year after the centenary of The Great Soul's birthday on 2 October 1869. It is now almost twenty-three years after that tragic day in January 1948 when the Mahatma was killed by the bullet of a fanatic. . . . [Today, in 1970] the unmitigated evil of the Apartheid system . . . has got its deadly grip on our society like a boa constrictor on its prey. Millions of people are insulted and humiliated and oppressed and denied their simplest human dignity simply because their skin color is [darker] than that of an oppressor who has lived under a moral wheelbarrow for too long. And many thousands of people who sympathize with Gandhi's belief in racial equality, in the common dignity of all men, are languishing in jail, in various forms of banishment, or in exile. . . . And so it may seem as if the Mahatma is, in fact, dead; and as if his spirit of greatness and compassion has really departed from us. But appearances are deceptive . . . [for] the Mahatma will never be dead. And in mourning Mohandas Karamchand Gandhi today we also celebrate his undying legacy to the world."

A Troubled Homecoming

Gandhi soon encountered other problems that had longer lasting consequences. First, the same brother who had run the family into debt was having some legal problems and asked Gandhi to use his influence with a powerful English colonial official, Charles Ollivant, whom Gandhi had met briefly in England. Gandhi asked Ollivant to pull some strings and quietly make his brother's problems go away, but the Englishman received this plea coldly and told him to go through proper channels. Gandhi realized that it would be unwise to make an enemy of Ollivant, but his pride had clearly been hurt. So the fledgling lawyer suddenly grew obstinate and bold and did not stop arguing his brother's case until Ollivant had him physically thrown out of the room.

Gandhi's feelings about the incident were mixed. On the one hand, he realized that he had made a powerful enemy needlessly and that he had been wrong to try to work outside official channels. Yet he also felt that he had been treated harshly and with disrespect. Shortly afterward he told a more experienced Indian lawyer that he wanted to complain to higher authorities; the lawyer told Gandhi that it would be wiser to ignore the insult, unless he wanted to risk never being able to practice law in India. So Gandhi swallowed his pride and abandoned the idea of filing a complaint. But he remained emotionally scarred at the thought that such a blatant injustice remained unchallenged.

The frustration and unhappiness of these early years back in India inevitably spilled over into Gandhi's home life. He had been in London so long that his four-year-old son, Harilal, barely knew him. In addition, Gandhi's marital conflicts with Kasturbai continued. He still insisted on trying to control every aspect of her existence, including pressuring her to go to school, and she still resisted. Later, a much more mature Gandhi concluded that his high-handed behavior toward his wife had been a mistake:

> My relations with my wife were still not as I desired. Even my stay in England had not cured me of jealousy. I continued my squeamishness and suspiciousness in respect of every little thing. . . . I had [also] decided that my wife would learn reading and writing and that I should help her in her studies, but . . . she had to suffer for my shortcoming. Once I went the length of sending her away to her father's house, and consented to receive her back only after I had made her thoroughly miserable. I saw later that all this was pure folly on my part.[16]

Mounting pressures at home and over his lack of work quickly overwhelmed Gandhi. As a result, in 1893, when a group of Muslim Indian businessmen from Porbandar offered him a job as a low-level lawyer in Britain's colony of Natal in South Africa, he jumped at the chance to make a fresh start. In April he said good-bye once again to Kasturbai, six-year-old Harilal, and also to a new baby son named Manilal.

The early years of Gandhi and Kasturbai's marriage were troubled due to Gandhi's attempts to control his wife's behavior.

HIS DISQUIETING JOURNEY

When Gandhi arrived in the South African city of Durban in May 1893, there were four European colonies in the region, two run by the British and two by the Dutch. The British ruled the Natal and Cape colonies while the Dutch Africans (commonly called

Boers or Afrikaners) ruled the Orange Free State and the Transvaal colonies. In all four of these colonial societies, divisions by color, class, religion, and caste created deep social divisions. White Christians, though composing a tiny minority of the population, made up the dominant socially and legally privileged class. Some 9 million native

Gandhi poses with his staff in South Africa, where he moved in 1893 to practice law.

blacks had almost no rights at all while residents of Indian origin, whom whites also looked down on, had some minimal though restricted rights.

Most Indians living in the South African colonies at the time had been brought there as indentured servants to provide cheap labor for the ruling whites. As a rule, after five years of service the Indians were freed and given a plot of land by the local government. A small minority of the Indian immigrants, however, had come on their own as merchants and had grown wealthy; it was from this elite local Indian group that Gandhi hoped to draw his clients.

Gandhi's ambitions were modest: to restart his career and in the process earn some money. But on a business trip shortly after his arrival, he soon ran afoul of the laws that restricted Indians' rights; the experience changed his life forever. His employer, Dada Abdullah Seth, wanted him to translate the Gujarati language, spoken by Indian court litigants in the Transvaal, into English. So Gandhi dutifully struck out for the Transvaal, taking the train tickets Seth had purchased for him and boarding a rail car at the Pietermaritzburg station in Durban. As Gandhi took his seat, a white man glared menacingly at the brown-skinned intruder. The man then turned on his heel and left. Minutes later the angry white man was back, with two railroad officials in tow. The officials told Gandhi to transfer to the car that was restricted for third-class passengers. When he protested that he had a first-class ticket and refused to leave, the officials summoned a policeman, who threw Gandhi off the train.

Embarrassed and angry, Gandhi waited in the station lobby for the next train. It was cold in the mountains, and his overcoat was in his luggage, which the station staff had confiscated because they saw him as a troublemaker. But rather than fight another battle over his coat, he shivered and brooded all night. In the morning he sent a long telegram of complaint to the general manager of the railways. Then he took another train, on which he traveled in third class unmolested.

Once in Pretoria, Gandhi learned that, again by tradition, European-owned hotels were reserved strictly for whites. When he finally found lodgings at one of the few American-owned hotels in the region (which was not so restrictive), he

A SOUTH AFRICAN HAILS GANDHI AFTER APARTHEID'S ABOLITION

Nelson Mandela, the former president of South Africa who led the movement to end apartheid, presented the Freedom of Pietermaritzburg Medal posthumously to Gandhi. This portion of Mandela's speech is excerpted from the African National Congress website.

"Gandhi's magnificent example of personal sacrifice and dedication in the face of oppression was one of his many legacies to our country and to the world. He showed us that it was necessary to brave imprisonment if truth and justice were to triumph over evil. The values of tolerance, mutual respect, and unity for which he stood and acted had a profound influence on our liberation movement, and on my own thinking. They inspire us today in our efforts of reconciliation and nation-building. . . . When municipalities and communities form a partnership . . . when each sector of society joins hands with the police to fight crime and violence; when the private sector and organized labor work together to promote growth and job opportunities, we all reap the benefits of the unity espoused by Gandhi."

was asked to dine in his room because his presence in the dining room might upset the other guests, many of whom were Europeans. A weary Gandhi agreed; but later the proprietor returned and said the other guests had agreed that Gandhi could join them in the dining room. In this single disquieting journey, Gandhi had experienced what seemed to him a puzzling quirk about South African society. He learned that bigotry against Indians was second nature to some whites while others found the prevailing discrimination embarrassing and were quite willing to accept Indians as equals.

A SOCIAL REFORMER IS BORN

The discrimination that twenty-four-year-old Mohandas Gandhi had experienced gnawed at him. Although he had planned to return home to India once the case he was working on was concluded, he was so deeply troubled by the anti-Indian prejudice in the British and Dutch colonies of South Africa that he decided to stay and work toward ending the mistreatment of Indians. A wealthy Indian merchant lent Gandhi his home and the young lawyer summoned Pretoria's Indian merchants to a meeting to decide on a strategy for attaining his goal.

On the evening of the meeting, the house's courtyard was packed with Indians who had come to hear Gandhi's first public speech. Still painfully shy, he was at first terrified; but as he made his way to the center of the crowd, his shyness suddenly dissolved. "I want to present you with the

facts of your condition," [17] he told his audience. Part of Gandhi's message that day was that Indians themselves were partly to blame for the discrimination against them. They should change themselves, he said,

Disturbed by the unfair treatment of Indians living in the British and Dutch colonies of South Africa, the young Gandhi resolved to remedy the situation.

by making sure always to conduct business ethically, adopting sanitary habits, forgetting the divisions of caste and religion, and learning fluent, precise English. He also stated his belief that Indians should adopt Western ways so that the Europeans could not say that they were backward and undeserving of equal treatment with whites. In addition, he strongly advised the group to use legal means to press their demands. "Remember that this is a far away land and that people will judge India by the way we behave," he told the assembled guests. "The best way to make the government change its attitude is to form an association to make petitions. If you agree with me, I shall be very happy to work for the association and do all I can to fight color prejudice." [18]

At the time, Gandhi was under the naive and decidedly mistaken impression that divisions between the two cultures would easily and gradually melt away. He did not yet understand how deeply most whites in South Africa felt threatened by Indians, who had arrived in the colonies as indentured servants and then stayed on as free, contributing members of society. Gandhi also did not see that out of this fear came the repressive, anti-Indian laws that he had seen in action when he first arrived.

These laws that Gandhi opposed extended far beyond the railways, however. In the British-controlled Natal Province, for example, Indians had to carry passes if they were out on the street after 9:00 P.M. In the Boer Orange Free State, Indians could not own property, engage in trade, or farm the land. Transvaal Indians had to pay a heavy tax for residency permits, even though they were only permitted to live in slums. And in parts of the Cape Colony, Indians were often prohibited from walking on pavements.

Gandhi stayed in Pretoria for a year, learning more about the lack of civil rights for Indians and petitioning the Boer government to change anti-Indian laws. Despite his diligent efforts, he won only one concession, however. Indians would be permitted to travel first class on trains—but only if they wore Western clothing.

FIGHTING FOR INDIANS' RIGHTS

Although his efforts had achieved only limited results, Gandhi had earned a reputation among Indians as a fair-minded attorney, mediator, and reform leader. In 1894 a group of Indian leaders in the Natal Province asked him to help them fight a proposed law that would take the right to vote away from the few Indians who had it. Gandhi agreed and formed an organization called the Natal Indian Congress (NIC). Many of the initial members wanted the organization to serve the needs of mainly well-to-do Indians who were Hindus, but Gandhi argued that this sort of discrimination was no better than the kind perpetrated by the whites. At his insistence, NIC welcomed all Indians—whether rich, poor, Hindu, Muslim, or Christian.

With the help of NIC members, Gandhi circulated petitions against the voting law among both Indians and whites, collecting some ten thousand signatures in all. The campaign did not, as he had hoped, stop passage of the law; but at least he had succeeded in mobilizing the Indian community of South Africa. NIC named Gandhi as its secretary, the organization's highest office. Over the next several months he worked tirelessly in that capacity, sleeping only a few hours each night. He was in ceaseless motion, writing eloquent newspaper articles about the plight of Indians in South Africa and working to expand the membership of NIC.

As time went on, NIC developed broader goals than just obtaining expanded rights for Indians. At Gandhi's urging, the organization worked to encourage greater harmony between Indians and Europeans. NIC also implored Indians to rediscover their own culture, yet at the same time promoted social reforms that sought to eradicate certain harmful ancient traditions still practiced by some Indians. For example, many in NIC opposed animal sacrifice, child marriage, and suttee, the practice of burning a widow alive on her husband's funeral pyre.

As NIC expanded beyond its upperclass origins, Gandhi worked hard to bring indentured servants and lower-caste Indians into the political fold. To expand the organization's appeal to these people, he tried to repeal a twenty-five-pound tax imposed on indentured servants who stayed in India after their terms of service were completed. The elite Indians knew that expanding the size of NIC lent the Indian community more power, so they reluctantly supported Gandhi's advocacy of indentured servants and other lower-caste Indians.

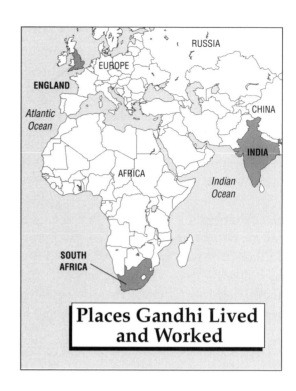

Places Gandhi Lived and Worked

Gandhi's reputation as a friend to the powerless grew. At the same time, membership in NIC skyrocketed after an incident in which a blood-covered indentured servant staggered into Gandhi's office seeking aid. The servant, whose name was Balasundaram, had been beaten savagely by his white master, after which he had run away. Even though the master was clearly abusive, for an indentured servant to run away was a criminal offense punishable by a prison sentence. Gandhi immediately took Balasundaram's case. Gandhi convinced a magistrate to charge Balasundaram's master with assault; and the master, faced with the prospect of jail, reluctantly agreed to release the injured man from indentured service. The situation was resolved, and Gandhi was seen as a hero by Indians all across South Africa.

RETURN TO INDIA

In South Africa, Gandhi had grown from a frustrated failure into a larger-than-life leader. In three years he had managed to mobilize a trampled minority into an influential political force. He had also found commercial success as a lawyer and used the fees he earned in his legal practice to finance more public activity. Yet he felt emotionally torn, for his family was in India while his work was clearly in Africa. In 1896, longing to see his wife and two sons, he set sail for Calcutta, India, with the intention of bringing them back to live with him in Africa.

Gandhi was unaware at the time that shortly after his departure new troubles for him, NIC, and South African Indians in general had begun to brew. A few months before, he had published a detailed account of Indian grievances against the colonial powers in South Africa. This list of grievances, which became known as the *Green Pamphlet*, had created a sensation among Indians and whites alike, and Gandhi had held out great hope that it would help the Indian cause. But in his present absence, its message was being distorted. Some whites who feared his growing power made certain that exaggerated accounts of the pamphlet's contents circulated among the majority of African whites, who came to believe that Gandhi wanted Indian colonists to launch an armed revolt against white rule.

Even as his words were upsetting people back in Africa, Gandhi himself was creating another stir in India. The bubonic plague had broken out in one district of Bombay. As poor sanitation was thought to spread the disease, Gandhi offered to inspect the latrines of the community and to write a report outlining the problem for the

GANDHI'S FAITH

Gandhi insisted that he was an average man and that anyone could accomplish what he had. He attributed his success to a dual faith in God and one's fellow human beings. This quote is excerpted from "Gandhiji's Writings" on the Itihaas website.

"I claim to be no more than an average man with less than average ability. . . . I have not the shadow of a doubt that any man or woman can achieve what I have, if he or she would make the same effort and cultivate the same hope and faith. Work without faith is like an attempt to reach the bottom of a bottomless pit. . . . My contribution to the great problem lies in my presenting for acceptance truth and *ahimsa* [nonviolence] in every walk of life, whether for individuals or nations. Nonviolence requires a double faith: Faith in God and also faith in man."

The untouchables, the lowest caste of Indians, were considered unworthy of attempts to eradicate the bubonic plague from their communities.

local government. The authorities agreed to this plan, but they insisted that the untouchables' homes were not worth investigating. Raw sewage was a problem there, the officials said, but they predicted that the untouchables would refuse to make changes. Gandhi thought that this claim was ridiculous and inspected the untouchables' homes anyway. Much to the embar-

rassment of the upper-caste Indians, he discovered that the latrines in the homes of the wealthiest Indians were dirtier than the latrines in the homes of the untouchables.

Gandhi had been in India for only a few months when he received a telegram from his friends in Natal asking him to return right away. The Natal Parliament (which comprised whites and held the real power in Natal) would soon convene, and its leaders were hostile toward NIC. On November 30, 1896, Gandhi set sail for Durban accompanied by his wife and sons. On the ship, the SS *Courland*, and on another vessel, the SS *Naderi*, were eight hundred Indians traveling to find work in South Africa. The passengers had no inkling that they and their fellow passenger, Gandhi, were headed straight into a political storm. In South Africa, the distorted message derived from his *Green Pamphlet* had convinced white militants that Gandhi had recruited the eight hundred Indian passengers to overrun the country with rebellious indentured servants!

3 Gandhi's Stormy Return to South Africa

As the *Courland*, carrying Gandhi, and the SS *Naderi* approached Durban harbor in mid-December 1896, the local authorities denied both ships entry to the docks. The official excuse was that the ships were under medical quarantine; the true reason, however, was that a mob of white militants, who were waiting on the docks, adamantly opposed both the immigration of any more Indians into Natal and the return of Gandhi the "troublemaker." The militants viewed the Indians and their leader as menaces bent on overthrowing white rule, and local officials were anxious to avoid any bloodshed.

After twenty-three days of quarantine, the ships were finally allowed to dock on January 13. Gandhi sent his family in a carriage to a friend's house. He refused, however, to allow the threat of violence to dictate his own actions and set off for the house on foot. It did not take long for a mob of whites to spot him, close in on him from all sides, pelt him with bricks and rotten eggs, knock his turban off, and punch him repeatedly. Luckily for Gandhi, the police arrived and were able to beat back the mob and protect him until he reached the house where his

family had gone. As night fell, however, another angry crowd gathered outside and screamed for his blood. Concerned for the safety of the man who owned the house, as well as the safety of his family, Gandhi dressed himself as a police officer and managed to escape. Ironically, the police superintendent created a diversion for Gandhi by leading the crowd in a song with the chorus: "Hang Old Gandhi on the Sour Apple Tree."[19]

The furor eventually died down. Shortly afterward Gandhi published an article in the *Natal Advertiser*, the newspaper read by local whites, clarifying the meaning of the *Green Pamphlet* and explaining that the Indians who had just arrived posed no threat to the colony. In a gesture of reconciliation, he declined to press charges against his attackers, which further helped to calm tensions. It was also an early example of his nonviolent reaction to violence.

However, Gandhi's use of nonviolence did not deter him from pursuing active campaigns against any legislation that restricted Indians' rights in South Africa. He had become a driven man, consumed by the idea that he had truth on his side and that he, the African Indians, and their cause would eventually prevail. "He never slacken[ed] or miss[ed] a trick," one biographer, Geoffrey Ashe, wrote later. "He [went] on and on, factually, lucidly, with a fearful staying power and meticulousness of detail. His strength [did] not come from religious ardor as usually understood . . . but from dedication to his Truth, a dedication that [would] not let him rest."[20]

A Brief Alliance with the British

Gandhi soon found this dedication—to what he saw as the truth and also to serving the cause of his fellow Indians—sorely tested in the wake of a new crisis, one larger than any he had so far encountered. In 1899 what later became known as the Boer War broke out in South Africa. It was waged between the British and the white Dutch Boers, who had lived in the Transvaal long before the British had arrived in Africa. The war started when Britain claimed and asserted its jurisdiction in the Boer colonies and the irate Boers immediately resisted. In this battle over which imperial power would control South Africa, Gandhi at first sympathized with the Boers' claim that Britain's actions were unjustified and imperialistic; but he could not in good conscience openly denounce the British, for he still

British soldiers fire a machine gun at the Boers during the Boer War. The war erupted in 1899 as the British and Dutch struggled for dominance in South Africa.

wore British clothing, taught the British national anthem to his children, and believed that Indians should uphold the same laws and work toward attaining the same rights as British citizens. In short, he felt as much a part of British civilization as he did Indian culture. So in the end, he felt compelled to support the British in the war. But he was determined to do so nonviolently.

As a way of supporting the British war effort, Gandhi proposed establishing an ambulance corps staffed with Indians. Many in the British army thought the idea was preposterous, saying that Indians were unreliable and worthless. But Gandhi persisted and the Indian Ambulance Corps was established in 1899, with Gandhi as its leader. The corps boasted a thousand free and indentured Indians, who consistently proved themselves heroic under fire. The goodwill that Gandhi and his ambulance drivers generated between the British soldiers and the Indians would prove to be useful in the future.

Three years of warfare left the British in control of South Africa. In gratitude for his service, the British awarded Gandhi the prestigious War Medal. This warming of relations so encouraged him that he actually believed his work in South Africa was finished. On October 18, 1901, he sailed with his family for India, determined to fight for Indians' rights in his native land, just as he had in his adopted land of Africa. Before he left, he promised to return to South Africa if NIC felt it needed his help in the future.

RENEWING AN OLD STRUGGLE

Gandhi returned to India to find that a new organization, the Indian National Congress (INC), was giving voice to the growing opposition among Indians to British rule. Gandhi visited a session of the congress in Calcutta, but he was immediately disappointed to find that it was more like a debating society than a political body that could effect any real reforms. Seeing an opportunity to turn the new organization into a force for change, Gandhi volunteered to be its secretary. Through a friend, the politician Gopal Krishna Gokhale, Gandhi pushed a resolution through the INC that supported complete civil rights for Indians in South Africa. This was intended partly as a statement of the congress's moral position and also as a message to the British that the organization considered itself important enough to work for Indians' civil rights outside as well as inside India.

In addition to aiding the INC, Gandhi turned his attention to a humanitarian cause that he felt had been neglected by British and Indians alike, namely the horrendous living conditions endured by India's lower castes. He created an uproar by personally cleaning one of the foul-smelling toilet rooms that served the members of the congress, a job usually relegated to untouchables. This unexpected and decidedly menial act by so famous and respected an Indian leader succeeded in drawing public attention to the plight of the untouchables and other socially repressed Indians. Ignoring this uproar, Gandhi immediately created another.

A Code to Live By

Gandhi had become a politician, but he remained a spiritual seeker. Although he had been a devout Hindu for years, he had begun to realize how much Hindu and Muslim beliefs had in common. But he also became a student of several Christian sects, including the Catholics, the Methodists, and the Quakers. In addition, he was greatly influenced by the Russian author Leo Tolstoy, who renounced force as a means of opposition. A group of Trappist monks and nuns who lived on a jointly owned farm outside of Durban also impressed Gandhi. He visited their community and called it a model village. To him, the Trappists' simple lifestyle was the ideal merger of God-centered beliefs and practical lifestyles. They served the local poor, grew their own food, made their own clothes, prayed for many hours, took vows of silence, and did without luxuries. Increasingly, Gandhi embraced similar practices.

Deciding to travel around India to inspect living conditions in other regions, he surprised Gokhale and other Indian leaders by insisting on traveling in third-class railcars; no other educated Indian had ever done such a thing.

If Gandhi had tried such tactics a few years before, he would have quickly alienated the well-to-do and powerful Indians whose help he desperately needed to forge a successful movement against British rule. But by now he had acquired the public image of an incorruptible moral authority as well as a political leader. Upper-class Indians seemed to sense that the unique combination of these roles within this one man could reach out and touch a public nerve and thereby prove a potent force for change; they were therefore willing to tolerate, and in fact eventually came to welcome, his periodic demonstrations and crusades to aid the poor and downtrodden.

As for Gandhi himself, his efforts to help oppressed Indians were never politically motivated. He later wrote in his autobiography that the poor, dirty, crowded masses of India revealed to him on his cross-country trip deeply depressed him. He was distressed, he said, by the many filthy temples, impoverished priests, and Indian aristocrats who lived in great luxury while peasants struggled nearby in squalor. Rich and cynical, many of the Indian elite held posts in the colonial government that were awarded by the British, but they did little actual work. These discoveries about his native country made Gandhi feel more strongly than ever that India needed widespread reforms, including the termination of British rule as well as the end of social injustices imposed by Indians on other Indians.

GANDHI'S GROWING IDEALISM

To his disappointment, however, Gandhi found that these crusades would have to be postponed. After he had spent less than a year in India, the Natal Indian Congress asked him to return to Africa immediately. And true to his earlier promise to NIC, he immediately sailed for Natal, taking his family with him.

What Gandhi found on his arrival in Africa late in 1902 was disheartening, for the goodwill between the British and Indian communities that had existed at the end of the Boer War had faded away. This was because British authorities, for political and economic reasons, were more interested in reestablishing good relations with the Boers than in improving social conditions for nonwhites. In fact, the British and Boers had recently joined forces to persecute African Indians more vigorously than ever before. Gandhi wanted to respond to this heightened animosity to Indians, but, recognizing the need to support his family, he first took the time to establish his law practice; he and his family moved to Johannesburg (in the Transvaal), where his new practice thrived.

Gandhi soon found himself a wealthy man, at least by the living standards of local African Indians (which were considerably lower than those for white Europeans). But he had not forgotten his commitment to the cause of Indians' civil rights. To further this cause, he used the first profits from his law

practice to establish an English-language weekly newspaper in Johannesburg called *Indian Opinion*. The editor, Mansukhlal Nazar, one of Gandhi's many devoted followers, worked without pay, but Gandhi himself was the real force behind the paper. As Gandhi's fame grew in the world outside the African Indian community, a skilled white printer named Albert West came from England to help. West was one of several Europeans who ended up spending their entire adult lives working, living, and protesting with Gandhi. West's loyalty was so deep that during a time of financial problems at the paper, he wrote, "I shall try to put things right as best I can. I [will] remain on, whether there is profit or not."[21]

Running his newspaper, in addition to practicing law, kept Gandhi constantly busy; yet he wanted to do even more to help his fellow Indians in their struggle for civil rights. He still supported British rule of South Africa, yet he believed that Britain needed to accord Indians the same respect and rights that it did white Europeans. He had also studied nonviolent reform movements in India, China, Russia, and America, and he concluded that nonviolent protest could achieve the political reforms he sought.

One of the goals he developed as part of his nonviolent approach to change was to demonstrate that people who shared and owned in everything equally could live in harmony and peace. Such a social structure, Gandhi thought, abolished "the eternal conflict between capital and labor." He wrote, "It means the leveling down of the few rich in whose hands is concentrated the bulk of the nation's wealth . . . and the leveling up of the semi-starved naked millions on the other."[22] To demonstrate this philosophy to Indians and whites alike, in June 1904 Gandhi took the audacious step of moving *Indian Opinion* and its employees to a new community in Durban, Natal. He called the communelike settlement Phoenix Farm and welcomed all castes and classes of Indians and Europeans to live there. The settlement never attained a large population, but the people it did attract represented a number of different races and religious backgrounds.

THE ZULU REBELLION

Phoenix Farm and some of Gandhi's other ideas and endeavors may have been idealistic at the time. Yet in the coming months and years, Gandhi often balanced such idealism with the same brand of hands-on political and social activism that he had employed in the past both in Africa and in India. In 1906, for example, as a humanitarian gesture, he organized another ambulance corps for the British. This time they were fighting the Zulus, a large tribe of African blacks who had rebelled against white rule.

Gandhi's experience with this relatively small six-month-long war was pivotal in his ongoing attempt to find a practical way of using nonviolence to resolve conflicts. During the fighting he witnessed the brutal methods employed by British soldiers against the Zulus, including the merciless flogging of unarmed prisoners. He later recalled,

The Zulu "rebellion" was full of new experiences and gave me much food for thought. The Boer War had not brought home to me the horrors of war with anything like the vividness that the "rebellion" did. This was no war but a man-hunt. . . . To hear every morning reports of the soldiers' rifles exploding . . . in innocent [Zulu] hamlets . . . was a trial. . . . The work of my ambulance corps consisted only in nursing wounded Zulus. I could see that but for us the [injured] Zulus would have been uncared for.[23]

Seeing such atrocities not only lessened Gandhi's respect for the British, for whom he still felt some lingering affinity and loyalty, but also greatly strengthened his intolerance for violence and his commitment to nonviolent protest.

The Zulu uprising was also a turning point for Gandhi because it made him think more deeply than ever about the relationship between his personal life and his duties as a leader. During these months he came to realize that his effectiveness as a leader might increase significantly if he committed himself to *brahmacharya*. This traditional Hindu vow of celibacy was designed to make a person more focused and self-reliant by eliminating the distractions of normal physical desires. "I pondered over *brahmacharya*," he later wrote,

and my convictions took deep root. . . . I clearly saw that one aspiring to serve humanity with his whole soul could not do without it. . . . [I realized] that I

Members of the Zulu tribe hold a meeting. In 1906, the Zulus rebelled against the British, who retaliated with a brutality that horrified Gandhi

should find myself unequal to the task if I were engaged in the pleasures of family life and in the propagation and rearing of children. In a word, I could not live both after the flesh and the spirit.[24]

Later in 1906, after more soul-searching, Gandhi took this vow. Although he and Kasturbai remained husband and wife and continued to work together, they no longer had sexual relations; and she shouldered most of the duties of raising the children, thus allowing him to devote more time and energy to his causes.

VOWING TO FIGHT THE BLACK ACT

Having made this major personal sacrifice in an effort to make himself a more effective leader, Gandhi tackled the next hurdle in the fight for Indians' rights. Indians were the predominant Asian minority in South Africa, but new discriminatory laws made life for them increasingly difficult. In March 1907, for example, the Transvaal government passed the Asiatic Registration Law, which required that all Indian men, women, and children be fingerprinted. Failure to register—or to deliver proof of registration on demand—resulted in fines, beatings, and jail time. Under the law's provisions, police could ask for the documents at any time, without warning or reason, and could enter private houses without permission of the occupants.

This law, which the local Indians came to call the Black Act, inspired Gandhi to organize a mass protest meeting that drew three thousand Indian men. In a speech he explained the content of the Black Act, then he proposed that Indians refuse to obey the law and be ready to suffer the penalties. Speaker after speaker leapt up to voice his support of noncooperation with the law. One such speaker, Sheth Haji Habib, passionately declared that the Indian men should swear an oath before God to disobey the law no matter what the consequences. Such an oath was obviously a solemn matter, and after a few moments of silent reflection, Gandhi rose to address the assembly and remind them of the hardships that surely lay ahead. "We shall go on till we succeed," he said.

It is quite possible that some of those who pledge themselves may weaken at the very first trial. We may have to remain hungry and suffer from extremes of heat and cold. Hard labor is likely to be imposed upon us in prison. We may even be flogged by [our jailers]. Or we may not be imprisoned, but [be] fined heavily and [have] our property attached and held up to auction for non-payment. Though some of us are wealthy today, we may be reduced to poverty tomorrow. We may even be deported from South Africa for good. . . . Our wisdom therefore lies in pledging ourselves, knowing full well that we shall have to suffer things like these. . . . Provided the entire community manfully stands the test, the end will be soon. But if many of us fall back under stress of trial, the struggle will be prolonged. At the same time I can boldly declare that so long as there is even a handful of men true to their pledge, there can only be one end to the struggle, and that is victory.[25]

Gandhi's speech was greeted with reverential silence instead of cheering. Then, as one, rapt audience members raised their arms over their heads and took the oath to defy the Black Act.

THE INVENTION OF SATYAGRAHA

The movement Gandhi now led employed what was often called passive resistance. But there was nothing passive about Gandhi's methods, and he came to detest the term. Gandhi wanted a new word to describe his vision of nonviolent resistance, and after much thought he settled on *satyagraha* ("the force of truth and love"). At the same time, he devised new ways to implement the satyagraha concept and further refined his philosophy to embrace civil disobedience. That meant breaking an unjust law, but doing so in a civilized manner that won the opposition's respect. The protesters hoped their civility and commitment would make officials in power realize that their cause was just. As always, Gandhi's unshakable goal was, through perseverance and strength of

TEACHING NONVIOLENCE

Gandhi often gave his followers instructions for practicing nonviolent satyagraha. Sometimes his advice took the form of written lists, such as this one from his essay "Young India," which is excerpted from Gandhi's Selected Writings.

"1. A satyagrahi [i.e., a civil resister] will harbor no anger.

2. He will suffer the anger of the opponent.

3. In so doing he will put up with assaults from the opponent, [and] never retaliate; but he will not submit, out of fear of punishment or the like, to any order given in anger.

4. When any person in authority seeks to arrest a civil resister, he will voluntarily submit to the arrest, and he will not resist the attachment or removal of his own property, if any, when it is sought to be confiscated by authorities.

5. If a civil resister has any property in his possession as a trustee, he will refuse to surrender it, even though in defending it he might lose his life. He will, however, never retaliate.

6. Non-retaliation excludes swearing and cursing.

7. Therefore a civil resister will never insult his opponent. . . .

8. A civil resister will not salute the Union Jack [the British flag], nor will he insult it or officials, English or Indian.

9. In the course of the struggle, if anyone insults an official or commits an assault upon him, a civil resister will protect such official or officials from the insult or attack even at the risk of his life."

will, to bring about a change of heart in his opponents. "Satyagraha thrives on repression," he later wrote, "till at last the repressor is tired of it and the object of Satyagraha is gained. A satyagrahi loves his so-called enemy even as he loves his friend. He owns no enemy. Strength does not come from physical capacity. It comes from an indomitable will."[26]

The first test of satyagraha was the organized opposition to the Black Act in the Transvaal. Most Indians simply refused to register and be fingerprinted at the offices the government had set up. In addition, satyagraha volunteers picketed these offices. And when the police attacked them with clubs, the protesters remained steadfastly nonviolent. Tyrants, Gandhi told them, will be defeated if the people show no fear in the face of their violence. By the end of July 1907, only a handful of Indians had registered in accordance with the Transvaal law.

The protests continued for months. In December, the Transvaal government lost patience and arrested Gandhi, along with other Indian leaders, on charges of failing to register. Gandhi pleaded guilty to the charges and even suggested a harsh sentence for himself and his companions. Accordingly, the judge sentenced them to two months of hard labor; as an added gesture of contempt, the jailers put Gandhi in a cell normally reserved for native black Africans.

Defying the Black Act brought Gandhi his first jail term, but it would not be his last. When the Indians heard of the sentence, many took to the streets and broke other minor laws in an effort to keep pressure on the government. Many illegally sold goods without the required peddler's license. These spontaneous protesters, whose ranks included both key Indian leaders and ordinary citizens, were arrested and the jails filled rapidly.

DEFYING THE LAW

Although prison conditions were harsh, Gandhi actually appeared to enjoy the isolation, which provided a welcome break from his hectic life. "I made myself quite comfortable in [jail],"[27] he later wrote. Such good cheer astounded General Jan Christian Smuts, the South African minister in charge of Indian affairs, who visited Gandhi's cell and proposed a deal. Smuts promised to repeal the Black Act and release imprisoned protesters if the Indians voluntarily registered. Gandhi agreed to these terms and called off the protest; however, some of his followers were angered by this deal and thought he had caved in too soon. In response, he explained that he believed in trusting everyone until they did something to prove they were untrustworthy.

As it turned out, General Smuts broke his promise. The Black Act remained in effect, and as a result, many Indians lost faith in satyagraha. But Gandhi remained undeterred. He bombarded General Smuts with appeals to keep his word and rescind the law; Gandhi also issued a bold call for all Indians who had trustingly registered to turn in their certificates of registration to their community leaders. Then

General Jan Christian Smuts promised to repeal the Black Act if the Indians registered, but he did not honor the agreement and the Black Act remained in effect.

he sent an ultimatum to the Transvaal government demanding repeal of the Black Act and promising that if the government refused to take action by August 16, 1908, many protesters would publicly burn their registration certificates.

When the government failed to repeal the law, more than two thousand Indians gathered in Johannesburg at 4:00 P.M. on August 16 and placed their certificates in a large cauldron. Gandhi gave those in the crowd an opportunity to back down, telling them that any person who wanted his certificate back should take it and go about his business. But no one came forward, and the entire crowd began demanding that the certificates be burned. Paraffin was poured over the mass of paper and a match was applied, in a sense both figuratively and literally rekindling the flame of satyagraha.

Gandhi knew that he must keep up the pressure on the government. Following the burning of the certificates, he encouraged emigrants from Natal to enter the Transvaal without the required papers. First one man tried to cross the border, then dozens, and over the course of the next few weeks some six thousand followed. The Indians crossing into the Transvaal illegally were arrested, tried, and sentenced to hard labor in prison. In October 1908 Gandhi himself was jailed for refusing to leave the Transvaal, but outside the prison walls the disobedience continued. In response, his jail term was extended from three to six months. Prison guards harassed him and forced him into cells with violent prisoners. Nevertheless, in May 1909 he emerged from jail still defiant and resumed his leadership of the movement.

THE AFRICAN INDIANS UNITE

Unfortunately for Gandhi and his followers, however, the authorities remained equally defiant and seemed even more determined to destroy the civil rights movement. In 1910 Britain formally unified the four colonies of the Transvaal, the Cape, the Natal, and the Orange Free State as the Union of South Africa. General Smuts, now the new nation's minister of finance and defense, remained Gandhi's formidable opponent. Another Boer, South African prime minister Louis Botha, joined Smuts in his attacks on Indians. Botha promised that he would "drive the coolies [his derogatory term for Indians] out of the country within four years."[28]

As the government adopted this hardline attitude, the former widespread sup-

port for protest among Indians began to dwindle. Meanwhile, Gandhi remained optimistic and bided his time, sure that the civil rights movement would once more gain steam. Sure enough, in an effort to harass Indians and induce them to leave the country, the Supreme Court of South Africa soon declared all Indian

Prime Minister Louis Botha took an aggressive stance against Indians, vowing to rid South Africa of the "coolies."

marriages invalid, a move that legally made all Indian children illegitimate. And just as Gandhi had expected, the protests erupted once again.

This time the voices of Indian women joined those of Indian men. Because the court's ruling directly affected the status of women, Gandhi planned to involve large numbers of Indian women in the nonviolent protests, and Kasturbai wanted to be among them. In the past she had not wanted to take an active role in her husband's protests, a desire that Gandhi carefully respected. Now that the well-being of Indian women was at stake, however, she actually demanded to be involved. Gandhi was pleased that Kasturbai wanted to participate, and on September 16, 1913, she and several hundred other women crossed the border into the Transvaal without the required permits. As expected, they were arrested and sentenced to three months in jail for trespassing. After this, many more women began participating in civil rights demonstrations.

The arrests of the women had the effect of further galvanizing Indians of all walks of life and inspiring them to new protests. When the male indentured laborers in Natal's gold mines learned that the women protesters had been arrested, they went on strike in support of them. Most of the Indians in South Africa were indentured laborers, and the nation depended on their work. Sensing an opportunity, Gandhi rushed to the mines and swiftly organized five thousand miners to march forty miles to the border to cross illegally, just as the women had done. These miners had been too frightened to fight the Black Act, but the arrest of the women, an offense they felt they could not forgive, gave them the courage to act. Not surprisingly, the government reacted harshly to the strike, arresting the miners and returning them to the mines. In the following weeks, they had to work under police escort for no pay and in prison uniforms and chains.

Instead of quashing the rebellion, however, the British actions only added more fuel to the fire. On November 6, led by Gandhi, nearly twenty-five hundred Natal protesters entered the Transvaal illegally. Gandhi was arrested twice on the march, but the authorities soon released him when they realized that only he could control the mob. At Balfour (a town in the Transvaal), the marchers, with the exception of Gandhi, were all arrested and herded onto three trains for shipment to prison in Natal.

Gandhi himself was arrested again on November 9, and this time he was sentenced to nine months of hard labor. As

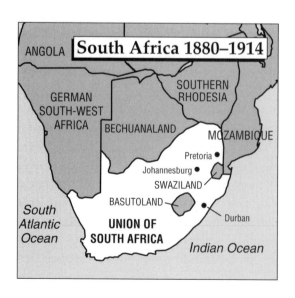

GANDHI ON WOMEN'S STATUS AND RIGHTS

Over the years, Gandhi developed a great respect for women and advocated equal rights and improved status for them. Near the end of his life, he had this to say to Margaret Sanger, the famous international advocate of birth control for women. His quote is excerpted from "Gandhiji's Writings" on the Itihaas website.

"My wife I made the orbit of all women. In her I studied all women. I came in contact with many European women in South Africa, and I knew practically every Indian woman there. I worked with them. I tried to show them they were not slaves either of their husbands or parents, not only in the political field but in the domestic as well. But the trouble was that some could not resist their husbands. The remedy is in the hands of women themselves. The struggle is difficult for them, and I do not blame them. I blame the men. Men have legislated against them. Man has regarded woman as his tool. She has learnt to be his tool and in the end found it easy and pleasurable to be such, because when one drags another in his fall the descent is easy."

the social unrest among Indians spread, he was unable to contain the fire from his prison cell. Miners were beaten by mounted military police, fifty thousand indentured servants went on strike, and when rioting broke out, the police opened fire, killing several protesters.

VICTORY

But to their surprise, government leaders soon found their brutal methods backfiring on them. The situation in South Africa had suddenly become world news, and the British drew harsh criticism from all quarters for their violent response to the protests. Among the international condemnations leveled at the South African government was a particularly

stern one from the British viceroy in India, who expressed "the sympathy of [all Indians], deep and burning . . . for their compatriots in South Africa in their resistance to . . . unjust laws." [29] Such rebukes, combined with the fact that the African Indian miners flatly refused to work, forced the South African government to give in. On December 18, 1913, the authorities released Gandhi early from his prison term.

To the government's dismay, the freed Gandhi immediately began organizing a new mass march, this one scheduled to start in Durban. In a surprising development, white railway workers chose the same time to go out on strike in hopes that the government would be more likely to meet their demands because of the turmoil caused by Gandhi's activities. This development caused Gandhi to employ logic that sometimes perplexed his followers. He announced that satyagraha never took advantage of an opponent's accidental difficulties; accordingly, he called off the upcoming march. Crippling South Africa was not his goal, he declared. The Black Act must be repealed, he maintained, but on the basis that the law was unjust, not because the government was overwhelmed with multiple problems. Gandhi's decision to call off the protest won him new respect worldwide. Messages of admiration came from England, India, and America. At the same time, public opinion around the world turned firmly against the South African government; in June 1914 the Black Act was finally repealed. Gandhi had proven that sometimes battles can be won by those who elect not to fight.

Once again, Gandhi concluded his work in South Africa and prepared to sail for India. When he and his family departed on December 19, 1914, General Smuts wrote, "The saint has left our shores; I hope for ever."[30]

Chapter

4 The Mahatma Comes Home

Gandhi had expected to work in South Africa only temporarily, but he had ended up staying for some twenty years. His fight there against laws that repressed Indians had made him, via news reports, a national hero in his native land. Once back in India, he intended immediately to begin pressing the British-controlled Indian government for similar reforms. But his first months at home turned out to be relatively quiet and uneventful. His old friend Gopal Krishna Gokhale advised him not to get involved in any reform movements for at least a year, suggesting that Gandhi should instead travel around India to get reacquainted with his country. Gandhi agreed, and for several months he visited remote corners of the country on crowded railway cars. Although he gave about forty speeches during his travels, he purposely refrained from saying things that might stir up trouble with the authorities.

The India that Gandhi got to know during these journeys was a rural, undeveloped nation peopled mostly by millions of uneducated workers and peasants. It was also a country of numerous languages, sects, and cultures. Gandhi realized that the middle and upper classes of India con-

stituted a tiny minority of the total population and that India's future lay not with this privileged few but with the masses who lived on the land. "Our salvation can come only through the farmer," he wrote. "Neither the lawyers, nor the doctors nor the rich landlords are going to secure it."[31]

By the end of his journey, Gandhi had adopted the simple dress of an Indian peasant in order to express his growing belief that India should not become completely westernized like England. He also knew that to help the illiterate and poor to understand that his cause and theirs was the same, he must dress in a way that they could understand. Wearing a loincloth and turban, therefore, he moved unnoticed among the masses.

In Ahmadabad, located near India's western coast, Gandhi accepted money from wealthy backers to start another communal settlement (like Phoenix Farm in South Africa), which Indians referred to as an ashram. As before, he hoped to set an example for his countrymen by creating a model of a peaceful community in which all members, regardless of caste, religion, or gender, worked together in harmony. To this end, twenty-five men,

As Gandhi adopted the simple clothing and lifestyle of a Hindu holy man, people came to view him as such and referred to him as Mahatma, or "Great Soul."

women, and children followed him from South Africa, set up housekeeping at the Sabarmati Ashram, and began living much like India's poor peasants. For the next sixteen years, Gandhi lived in the ashram in a single room the size of a prison cell. Kasturbai and their now four sons—Harilal, Manilal, Rramdas, and Devadas—lived at the ashram too, but because of Gandhi's vow of celibacy, they dwelled in separate quarters.

Because Gandhi had come to dress and live so simply and modestly, almost like a traditional Hindu holy man, more and more Indians began viewing him as a kind of saint. Soon people were calling him Mahatma, which means "Great Soul," a title formerly given only to greatly honored holy men. The Indian poet Rabindranath Tagore—who won the Nobel Prize for literature in 1913—helped to spread a sort of "Gandhi worship." Tagore called him "a Great Soul in peasants' garb."[32] Gandhi, however, objected to both the title and the worship, for he believed himself to be quite ordinary.

A Momentary Lapse into Anger

Gandhi was probably the only person in all of India who held this opinion, however. Indians far and wide and of all walks of life agreed with Tagore that the Mahatma was an extraordinary individual who had the potential to do great things for the country and its people. In addition, because of his fame and his growing saintly image, well-to-do Indians and whites alike saw the potential of boosting their personal prestige by associating with him in public. For these reasons he was constantly asked to comment on events in the news and to speak at various kinds of gatherings.

It was at such a gathering in February 1916 that Gandhi decided it was time for him to stop keeping such a low political profile. Annie Besant, a European woman who had embraced Hinduism, asked him to speak at the dedication of Benares Hindu University, which she had founded. In attendance at the dedication was the British viceroy, Lord Charles Hardinge, the highest ranking British official in India. The audience had expected to hear Gandhi praise Besant's college, but instead, he rose and gave a stinging rebuke of Indians who had grown comfortable under British rule. He blasted the conference speakers for using English, the language of a foreign race occupying India. "If . . . our languages are too poor to express the best thoughts," Gandhi said, "then I say that the sooner we are wiped out of existence the better."[33]

For Gandhi, such ideas were not new, but he expressed them with greater force and conviction than ever before. Then he suddenly seemed to step out of character, as both the content and tone of his speech became more hostile. He seemed to sympathize with bomb-throwing nationalists, for instance, and hinted that a dead viceroy might be a greater man than a living viceroy. As he spoke, rising tension in the audience gave way to complete

Lord Charles Hardinge (right), the viceroy of India, is pictured here with Britain's King George V.

pandemonium, and scattered cheers from radical Indian students were drowned out by angry cries from whites for him to sit down and be quiet.

Gandhi's seeming support of violence in his speech particularly disturbed some of his followers. He was, after all, the man who had written, "I believe that nonviolence is infinitely superior to violence. . . . Nonviolence is the law of our species [just] as violence is the law of the brute." [34] But these hostile remarks proved to be but a momentary lapse, provoked by Gandhi's growing impatience and restlessness. No longer satisfied to remain silent on political matters, he longed to lead the Indian masses on a mission, namely to end British rule in their country. Despite his momentary display of ill temper, which he came to regret (and which showed that he was indeed not a saint but a man), he felt himself ready to accomplish this lofty goal using his usual nonviolent methods. He would, he told a follower, endeavor to "pit the soul force against brute force." [35]

GANDHI GOES ON THE OFFENSIVE

But though Gandhi was ready to fight for independence, a temporary but important obstacle stood in his way. World War I, which had begun in 1914, was still in progress. Britain and its allies were at war with Germany and the Ottoman (Turkish) Empire, and the vast majority of Indians sympathized with the Allied cause. Moreover, on moral grounds Gandhi refused to take advantage of his opponent's trou-

bles. He insisted that Indians should support the British war effort, and he even recruited soldiers for that effort in 1918. In a letter, he told the viceroy where he stood: "I recognize that in the hour of its danger we must give ungrudging and unequivocal support to the Empire of which we aspire in the near future to be partners in the same sense as the [British] Dominions over seas." [36]

Even if Gandhi felt obliged to put his dispute with the British on hold, the opportunity to fight nonviolently for needed social and political change within India soon presented itself. In April 1917 Rajukumar Shukla, a poor farmer, approached Gandhi about a group of peasants and their grievances against their wealthy landlords. Gandhi agreed to travel with Shukla to Champaran, a district in the Himalayan foothills, where a million tenant farmers were being forced to pay higher rents to their landlords. Farmers who objected to the rent increase were beaten and their cattle were impounded. Under such duress, thousands had signed new leases agreeing to pay the increased rents.

When Gandhi began investigating the complaints, he was arrested and ordered to leave Champaran. His response was, to no one's surprise, consistent with his principle of satyagraha: He refused to leave and asked for the maximum punishment. Luckily for Gandhi, sensing that a jail sentence for such a famous man might create more problems than it solved, the judge dropped the case.

Now free to stay in Champaran for as long as he wished, Gandhi called in teachers and doctors to educate the peas-

GANDHI'S WEALTHY SUPPORTERS

Gandhi often spoke out against those who held great fortunes. However, he took money from the wealthy, including the multimillionaire G. D. Birla, whose contributions helped support Gandhi's causes and ashrams. In the on-line article: "Gandhi: Patron Saint of the Industrialist," author Leah Renold examines the two men's relationship and finds fault with Gandhi for not questioning Birla's business practices.

"With Birla's beneficence [generosity], Gandhi was able carry on his massive political campaigns, as well as to maintain a semblance of poverty and simplicity in lifestyle, while enjoying almost limitless financial resources. . . . Gandhi put forward the illusory image of poverty and simplicity while he was actually living very comfortably. We can only speculate whether this image-making was political posturing on Gandhi's part or whether the amenities were forced on him by the practicalities of operating a massive movement. . . . When Gandhi was questioned by the journalist Louis Fischer about the percentage of his budget which was funded by the rich, Gandhi admitted that practically all of it was, adding, 'In this ashram, for instance, we could live much more poorly than we do and spend less money. But we do not and the money comes from our rich friends.' These positions of Gandhi's do not seem to correspond to other elements in Gandhi's life and thought . . . [yet] Gandhi refrained from criticizing or questioning Birla."

ants' children and tend to the sick. Meanwhile, he relentlessly negotiated with the landowners, appealing to their sense of morality and fairness and promising never to leave them alone until they changed their position. These tactics proved effective, for after seven months they agreed to lower the rents.

As time went on, Gandhi increasingly used this tactic of appealing to his opponents' moral sense. In this regard, he regularly took advantage of the fact that he was famous, widely loved and respected, and seen as a unique kind of holy man or saint. By going on fasts, in which he threatened to starve himself to death if his demands were not met, he usually managed to shame his opponents into backing down. Simply put, whatever the political differences they may have had with him, most held him in a high degree of respect, often even in awe, and they did not want to be responsible for the suffering and death of the renowned Great Soul, lest their own souls be somehow imperiled.

One such Gandhian hunger strike occurred early in 1918 when he convinced textile mill workers in Ahmadabad to go on strike. When the Indian mill owners threatened to respond with violence,

Gandhi began a fast and invited the press to come and interview him as he rested on a string cot under a big shade tree near the mill. On the third day of Gandhi's fast, as he grew weaker and apparently thinner, the mill owners could no longer stand to see him suffer, especially with the press looking on, and they settled the strike.

Incidents such as this strike settlement, along with Gandhi's ceaseless work on behalf of India's poor, continued to strengthen his status as a national hero and spiritual figure. Devotion to the Mahatma soon grew to near-hysterical proportions in some parts of the country, as adoring crowds followed him nearly everywhere he went. His feet and legs were often scratched and bleeding because thousands prostrated themselves at his feet and reached out to grab him. Admirers traveled to his ashram from all over India, overjoyed merely to catch a distant glimpse of him; some Indians even considered him a reincarnation of God, like Buddha or Krishna. Gandhi himself remained mystified and at times visibly annoyed by all of this adoration. "I am no Mahatma," he insisted on one occasion.

> My Mahatmaship is worthless. It is due to my outward activities, due to my politics, which is the least part of me and is, therefore, evanescent [momentary and fragile]. What is of abiding worth is my insistence on truth, nonviolence and *bramacharya*, which is the real part of me. That part of me, however small, is not to be despised. It is my all. I prize even the failures

and disillusionments which are but steps towards success."[37]

Rather than fall at his feet, Gandhi wanted people to walk in his footsteps—or better yet, to walk beside him. He wanted their help, not their worship.

DIFFERING OPINIONS ON HOW TO ACHIEVE HOME RULE

The question many Indians and whites were asking at that moment was, in effect, Where exactly were Gandhi's footsteps leading? Late in 1918, World War I was finally drawing to a close and it seemed that the time was at hand for Gandhi to begin working for India's independence from Britain. A few Indian leaders wanted simply to declare independence, to drive out the British by force if necessary, and afterward to have nothing further to do with them. Gandhi, however, wanted both a peaceful transition of power and to maintain a working partnership with Britain. It would be in India's best possible economic and strategic interests, he maintained, for it to become one of the British "Commonwealth" nations—along with Canada, Australia, and New Zealand. These nations were fully independent but maintained close social and economic ties with Britain. At this time, Gandhi was still partly motivated by the lingering belief that the British Empire, with all of its faults and arrogance, had the potential to use its vast wealth and power as a force for spreading civilization and bringing peaceful solutions to international problems; and therefore that the most constructive course for India was to remain on friendly terms with the British during the transition to independence.

To this end, in a series of editorials Gandhi expressed his thoughts on how to achieve a sort of partnership with the British aimed at implementing Indian home rule. These editorials were then assembled in a small booklet entitled *Hind Swaraj*, or *Indian Home Rule*. "If we act justly," Gandhi wrote in the booklet, "India will be free sooner.

You will see, too, that if we shun every Englishman as an enemy, Home Rule will be delayed. But if we are just to them, we shall receive their support."[38]

In India, popular support for home rule was strong, although different factions promoted different strategies for achieving that goal. Some wanted to negotiate with the British government; others favored armed rebellion. Gandhi, on the other hand, advocated nonviolent noncooperation. "I believe," he said,

A crowd gathers around Gandhi's rickshaw. He was often mobbed by adoring crowds, and some even worshiped him as a reincarnation of God.

"that no government can exist for a single moment without the cooperation of the people, willing or forced, and, if people suddenly withdraw their cooperation in every detail, the government will come to a standstill."[39]

The British government was likewise divided about how to face the growing Indian nationalism. Some officials resisted any change in India's status and some favored an armed suppression of any protests or resistance. Others favored conferring political rights on India and making it a member nation of the British Commonwealth after the war. In England, one mem-

Indian protesters pose in front of a large figure representing British goods, which the demonstrators later burned. Gandhi advocated nonviolent protests such as this.

ber of Parliament, Sir Edwin Montague, supported a new policy toward India that would result in the "increasing participation of Indians in every branch of Government" and "self-governing institutions."[40]

This sort of conciliatory language by a respected British leader led a number of Indians to expect greater freedoms; but Britain's hard-liners soon won the debate over India's status. Instead of granting more liberty to its colony after World War I, Britain's policy toward India actually grew more repressive. In 1919 Parliament passed the Rowlatt Act, giving the Indian colonial authorities emergency powers to deal with "revolutionary" activities by imprisoning thousands of Indian nationalists and allowing no appeals.

Disappointed by this turn of events, Gandhi pleaded for the repeal of these policies, but to no avail. In keeping with the principles of satyagraha, he called for a national work stoppage, known in India as a *hartal*. When British leaders and other opponents accused him of being anti-British, Gandhi had a ready answer: "I am not anti-English," he wrote, "I am not anti-British; I am not anti–any Government; but I am anti-untruth, anti-humbug, and anti-injustice. So long as the Government spells injustice, it may regard me as its implacable enemy."[41]

A TURNING POINT

On March 30, 1919, the planned *hartal* began in the large northern city of Delhi; and a week later Indians across the entire country followed suit. At first, the work stoppage was peaceful. But Gandhi had never before tried to launch and maintain control of such a large protest. What is more, his nonviolent approach was hard for some of the angry people to understand and implement. For these reasons the protest deteriorated into arson, cut telegraph lines, looting, train stoppages, assaults on Englishmen, and other acts of violence.

A guilt-ridden Gandhi blamed himself for the disorders, believing that launching the movement before the people were ready had caused the violence. So he called off the *hartal* and fasted for three days. "My religion teaches me," he wrote, "that whenever there is distress which one cannot remove, one must fast and pray. . . . What the eyes are for the outer world, fasts are for the inner [world]."[42]

The fruits of Gandhi's tactical error were unfortunately bitter. On April 13, 1919, in the city of Amritsar, three prominent English businessmen were killed by an angry mob. In response, the British dispatched a high military commander, General Reginald Dyer, to take command of the situation. Dyer immediately issued a proclamation banning all public assembly in the town. But though the proclamation was read aloud in public places, the message failed to reach some parts of the city. When nearly 20,000 unarmed Indians gathered in a large vacant city lot, General Dyer arrived on the scene with his forces and without warning ordered his troops to open fire. The soldiers shot into the panicked crowd for ten minutes, discharging more than sixteen hundred rounds of ammunition. After ten minutes, 379 Indians were dead and 1,137 were wounded.

The Amritsar Massacre was a critical turning point for India, for it marked the beginning of the end of British authority there. The Indian people united behind Gandhi and the Indian National Congress (INC) in support of independence. And Gandhi responded to the massacre by calling for a widespread policy of noncooperation and a boycott of all British products. He also began editing two more newspapers committed to keeping the public abreast of current events: the Hindu language *Navajivan* and the English language *Young India*.

GANDHI RALLIES THE MASSES

To promote the noncooperation and boycotts he had called for, Gandhi toured the Indian countryside by train. Dressed only in a loincloth and a shawl, he called on his listeners to stop wearing British clothing, to shed their foreign clothes and disrobe on the spot, and finally to set fire to the mountains of clothes.

Not only should Indians not wear Western-style clothing, Gandhi stated, they should also dress only in clothes that had been produced from cloth spun by Indians. Everywhere he went he took a spinning wheel and he often spun yarn as he spoke to the crowds. He said that his spinning was a means of connecting to the Divinity, saying later, "I have described my spinning as a penance or sacrament. And, since I believe that where there is pure and active love for the poor there is God also, I see God in every thread that I draw on the spinning-wheel."[43]

But for Gandhi, the spinning wheel also symbolized resistance to British rule. India had once been self-sufficient in the production of *khadi*, a type of homespun cloth. But under British rule, the Indians had begun both exporting raw materials to England and importing cloth from England; and this had made the nation dependent on its colonial masters in order to clothe its people. Under Gandhi's guidance, spinning became a moral duty and homespun cloth became a symbol of self-sufficiency, self-pride, and independence. Susan Bean, an eminent American anthropologist, noted that there was a practical aspect to Gandhi's promotion of this seemingly backward technology:

> Like most leaders of the nationalist movement, Gandhi thought the industrialization of India to be of paramount importance, but unlike most of them he was opposed to mechanized industry, which he viewed as a sin perpetrated on the world by the West. He wanted to revive artistry. . . . [In his view] machines were laborsaving devices that put thousands of laborers out of work, unthinkable in India where the masses were under-employed. Factory production facilitated the concentration of wealth in the hands of a few capitalists, and transformed workers into "utter slaves."[44]

THE BURDEN OF LEADERSHIP

Millions of Indians responded to Gandhi's call for the country's inhabitants to make

Spinning was a religious experience for Gandhi, but he also valued its practical applications. Gandhi promoted spinning as a way of reducing India's unemployment and boosting its self-sufficiency.

their own clothes, and hundreds of thousands of Indians, at his urging, staged protests against the British authorities. By the end of 1921, some thirty thousand protesters and noncooperators were behind bars in Indian jails, including many INC party leaders. The congress, which by this time had grown into a well-organized and influential political party, was convinced that Gandhi should hold the reins of leadership during this critical time. Its leading members declared him

the organization's director and gave him complete executive authority, including the right of naming his own successor.

Gandhi soon found himself forced to use this new authority to defuse a serious crisis. Violence broke out in Chauri Chaura, a town in northern India. A group of protesters organized by the INC had begun a peaceful demonstration, but when the police taunted them, the protesters turned on the officers. Twenty-two policemen fired shots at

Gandhi (center) and members of the Indian National Congress. The INC, a pro-independence political party, named Gandhi their director.

the crowd, fortunately hitting no one, then hastily retreated to the police station. The mob proceeded to set the station on fire, and as the officers staggered out one by one, the protesters hacked them to pieces and threw their corpses into a raging bonfire.

This bloody incident convinced Gandhi that many of his followers were still not ready to engage in large-scale nonviolent demonstrations. Responding quickly to the riots, he canceled all scheduled protests and asked Indians everywhere to halt all violence against the British immediately. Once again, he began a fast, in this case to punish himself for his "mistake" of assuming that all of his followers understood the need to refrain from violence. Despite the fact that these moves by Gandhi succeeded in quelling the rioting, on March 10 the

GANDHI PLEADS GUILTY

At his trial in March 1922, Gandhi pled guilty to the charge of sedition and did not ask for mercy. Before the British judge sentenced Gandhi to six years in prison, he shook Gandhi's hand and said these words to the Mahatma, which are quoted in Taya Zinkin's The Story of Gandhi.

"It would be impossible to ignore the fact that, in the eyes of millions of your countrymen, you are a great patriot and a great leader. Even those who differ from you in politics, look upon you as a man of high ideals and of noble and even saintly life. . . . I do not forget that you have consistently preached against violence. . . . How you could have continued to believe that violence would not be an inevitable consequence [of all of this social and political protest], it passes my capacity to understand."

A photo taken on September 12, 1923, shows Gandhi serving his prison sentence.

government arrested him and charged him with sedition. On March 18, 1922, after having been found guilty, he was sentenced to six years in prison. At the sentencing hearing, he told the judge, "I am here to invite and cheerfully submit to the highest penalty that can be inflicted upon me for what in law is a deliberate crime."[45]

As it happened, events unrelated to politics intervened to shorten Gandhi's sentence. After serving nearly two years of his sentence, Gandhi became ill with appendicitis, and in February 1924, citing their concerns for his health, the authorities released him early. He found that during his incarceration the number of protests against the government had decreased significantly, presumably due to the absence of his full-time leadership. Hoping to keep the dream of independence alive, he resumed his full-time responsibilities and activities as leader of the INC.

However, Gandhi soon came to feel that neither his efforts as a politician nor the way his followers had come to treat him like a saint were helping the cause of Indian independence. Therefore, less than a year after retaking the reins of the congress, he announced his retirement from the job and scolded his countrymen for idolizing him so much. "I have never liked this reliance on me for everything," he said.

> It is the very worst way of managing national affairs. The Congress must not become, as it has threatened to become, one man's show, no matter how good or great that one man be. I

often think that it would have been better for the country and for me if I had served the full term of my imprisonment.[46]

A DARING NEW RESOLUTION

Believing that he had put politics behind him, Gandhi shifted his focus to building a strong, self-sufficient India. He called this process "purification" because its goal was to help the country rid itself of its dependence on British political and economic organization and to develop complete reliance on native political and economic organization and methods. "My belief," he wrote, "is that the instant India is purified, India becomes free, and not a moment sooner."[47] To help foster this process, Gandhi traveled all over the country setting up local Indian craft and cloth-spinning industries. Often these ventures required the outlay of some initial capital; and with his warm, impish smile he charmed a number of wealthy followers into supplying the needed money. At the same time, he was not shy about asking for even the smallest contributions to support the cause of making India self-reliant. Once someone asked him for an autograph for an American friend and he answered with a grin, "If you give me twenty rupees."[48] Although the autograph-seeker offered only half that amount, Gandhi signed anyway.

Gandhi was well aware that, while he was dutifully conducting these relatively quiet campaigns, social and political unrest was brewing in many parts of

India. He knew that if he, as the recognized leader of the movement for independence, chose to embrace violent revolution, the country would readily begin a bloody fight. But his commitment to satyagraha remained firm. It became clear to him that in order to ensure the use of nonviolent methods and thereby to avert possible bloodshed, he would have to reenter politics whether he liked it or not. In December 1928 he reluctantly began once more to take an active role in the deliberations and activities of the INC.

By this time most of the leaders of the congress, having grown increasingly impatient for major change, were ready to begin acting more boldly than ever before. At a December meeting of the body in Calcutta, Gandhi was among the leaders who endorsed a daring and potentially risky new resolution. It said that if Britain did not grant India the status of an independent British Commonwealth nation by the end of 1929, the congress would organize a countrywide campaign of noncooperation. Indians everywhere would refuse to pay their taxes, and that surely would bring the government grinding to a halt. The acceptance of this resolution set the stage for a major confrontation with Britain.

Chapter

5 The Road to Independence

On December 31, 1929—the deadline the Indian National Congress had given the British for granting India its independence—India was still firmly under British rule. Most congress leaders wanted to carry through their threat to launch a campaign of noncooperation, particularly one involving refusal to pay taxes; however, they had not yet reached agreement on exactly how to organize the protests or on which taxes to target. Thus, they turned to Gandhi to come up with an effective plan.

The first step in the plan was to declare January 21, 1930, India's Independence Day and to invite all Indians to take what Gandhi called the "Independence Pledge." The pledge consisted of a denouncement of British rule and a vow to carry out the instructions of the INC regarding the manner and dates of organized protest. Several million Indians took the pledge, soon after which Gandhi proceeded with the next step of the plan. On March 1 he delivered a letter to Lord Irwin, the latest British viceroy, detailing why he felt the British system was crushing the life out of the Indian people. A perfect example of British tyranny, Gandhi wrote, were the British salt laws, which made it a punishable crime for

Indians to make their own salt or possess salt not purchased from factories run by the government. In the letter, Gandhi promised to violate the salt laws if the viceroy did not act within eleven days. This was the first time that he had publicly expressed outright opposition to British rule, and he went so far as to call it a "curse";

> And why do I regard the British rule as a curse? It has impoverished the dumb millions by a system of progressive exploitation and by a ruinous expensive military and civil administration which the country can never afford. It has reduced us politically to serfdom. It has sapped the foundations of our culture. And by the policy of cruel disarmament, it has degraded us spiritually . . . [and] seems to be designed to crush the very life out of [the poor]. Even the salt he [the poor Indian] must use to live is so taxed as to make the burden fall heaviest on [the poorest]. . . . I respectfully invite you to pave the way for the immediate removal of these evils, and thus open a way for a real conference between equals.[49]

THE SALT MARCH

The viceroy, very unwisely it turned out, did not respond to the letter. So on March 12, Gandhi, accompanied by seventy-eight followers, began marching from the Sabarmati Ashram toward the coast of the Arabian Sea, some two hundred miles away. Each day they walked about twelve miles in the tropical heat, and Gandhi, now sixty-one, set an unusually brisk pace. Because his appeal to the British viceroy had been widely distributed and had become international news, the villagers who lived along the route were expecting the marchers. These peasants decorated their homes festively, sprinkled the dusty roads with leaves, then fell to their knees as the marchers passed. At least twice daily, the marchers halted for an open-air meeting where the Mahatma preached his familiar message—namely, to make homespun cloth, shun alcohol and drugs, and lead pure lives.

Surrounded by fellow protesters, Gandhi leads the salt march of 1930. Gandhi began the march in the Sabarmati Ashram with seventy-eight followers and ended at the Arabian Sea coast with thousands.

Before long, the ranks of the marchers began to swell. First, three hundred head-men of villages quit their government jobs and joined the march. Then, from all over India young people, peasants, and even wealthy aristocrats joined the throng, along with representatives of the press who were covering the momentous event in its entirety. Meanwhile, several residents of each village accompanied the marchers to the next village like an honor guard. By the time the marchers reached the coast near Dandi on April 5, they were several thousand strong; yet British officials expressed little concern and disdainfully called the protest a ridiculous publicity stunt.

Then came the climax of the march—its principal act of protest against the British. On April 6, after a sleepless night of prayer, Gandhi calmly walked to the mud flats at the edge of the sea, where the tide had recently gone out. He picked up a few grains of salt left by the waves. "Watch," he said, with the news reporters listening raptly. "I am giving a signal to the nation."[50] It was a simple act, but it symbolized the defiance of hundreds of millions of Indians against the world's strongest colonial power.

SATYAGRAHA WORKS

Inspired by the salt march and Gandhi's symbolic gesture, Indians of all walks of life joined in similar nonviolent protests. In violation of British law, native salt-making exploded across the country. Along the Indian seacoasts, for example, peasants waded into the water with pots and pans to evaporate seawater and make illegal salt. Even the INC got into the act; on the roof of the congress party headquarters in Bombay, police found a huge salt-making operation and subsequently arrested many congress members. As news of the raid on INC headquarters spread, sixty thousand protesters assembled in the nearby streets. The police hauled them away by the hundreds, tied together with long ropes. Soon one hundred thousand people were in prison; meanwhile, in Bombay another two hundred thousand protesters marched in the streets, denouncing the British and calling for them to leave India.

During this time, Gandhi kept himself closely informed about the protests, arrests, and both British and worldwide reaction to these events. Taking advantage of all the attention, on May 4 he announced plans to lead a protest march on the government-run Dharsana Salt Works north of Bombay. Learning of his intentions, the authorities quickly arrested him and threw him in a prison cell; but his followers, led by the female Indian poet Sarojini Naidu, dutifully carried out the plan.

At the salt works near Bombay, twenty-five hundred volunteers, including Gandhi's son Manilal, arrived to face muddy ditches, barbed wire, and four hundred native policemen led by six British officers. As the front rank of twenty-five marchers peacefully approached the barrier, several officers armed with large wooden sticks stepped forward and rained blows on their heads. Following Gandhi's explicit instructions not to fight back, the protesters did not even raise their arms to protect them-

Inspired by the salt march, young supporters of Gandhi take seawater in vessels to create their own salt. All along India's coasts, people carried out similar demonstrations to protest the salt laws.

selves but just fell to the ground, after which the police threw them into ditches. Then another group of twenty-five protesters advanced and was beaten down; and then another, and still another until all twenty-five hundred protesters had submitted to the police beatings.

At last, satyagraha had worked exactly as Gandhi had envisioned that it should and could. International reporters had witnessed the event, and they relayed their accounts of the brutality against peaceful demonstrators to a stunned world. Public officials and newspaper editorials from many quarters of the globe denounced the actions of the British authorities; in London's *Manchester Guardian*, the poet Tagore echoed the feelings of many when he wrote that Britain had "completely lost her formal moral prestige in Asia. She is no longer regarded as the champion throughout the world of fair dealing."[51]

THE BRITISH MAKE A DEAL

Indeed, the salt march succeeded in changing Britain's policies toward India. The British were deeply embarrassed by this widely publicized brutality that had been perpetrated by police officers under their control. At home in Britain, several noted politicians read accounts of the salt march demonstration in the London papers and publicly stated their support for Gandhi and Indian home rule. In addition, British prime minister Ramsay MacDonald received telegrams from around the world asking for the Mahatma's release from prison. Partly at MacDonald's urging, Gandhi was freed on January 26, 1931, along with the members of the INC who had been arrested for making salt.

Once freed, Gandhi met with the British viceroy, Lord Irwin, who was finding it difficult to maintain law and order in India. Winston Churchill, then an influential member of Britain's Parliament, believed that by granting an audience to Gandhi, the British viceroy was unwisely making a first move toward India's independence. Churchill found both Gandhi's tactics and success infuriating. He fumed over the "nauseating and humiliating spectacle of this one-time Inner Temple lawyer, now seditious fakir [self-proclaimed Hindu or Muslim holy man], striding half-naked up the steps of the Viceroy's palace, there to negotiate and parley on equal terms with the representative of the [British] King-Emperor."[52]

Despite Churchill's opposition, Viceroy Irwin and Gandhi agreed to a deal in February 1931. The Irwin-Gandhi pact prom-

In a photo dated February 24, 1931, Gandhi bows his head to acknowledge the cheers of his supporters following his release from prison.

ised that if Indians halted the civil disobedience, the British government would release the one hundred thousand Indians jailed during the salt protests. The viceroy also granted permission for Indians to make salt along the seacoast and invited the Indian National Congress to send a representative to London to discuss India's future status. It must be emphasized that Viceroy Irwin did not promise independence for India, and some Indians criticized Gandhi for not achieving enough from these negotiations. But Gandhi's perspective was different. He felt the pact was the first step in a changing relationship with Britain that eventually would lead to India's independence.

A GOODWILL MISSION

Gandhi's assessment had been essentially right. The next major step in the changing relationship between Britain and India occurred on August 20, 1931. Gandhi traveled to London as the sole representative of the INC to the Round Table Conference, the second of two meetings Parliament held to discuss the future of India. He tried to explain his desire for Britain to grant India independence voluntarily, without the need for any more protests and certainly without the need for any sort of bloodshed. In addition, Gandhi appealed to the moral sense of British leaders. To Sir Samuel Hoare, the secretary of state of India, he explained that his concern was for the British as well as Indians. "One must hate sin but . . . love the sinner," Gandhi said. "I think it is just as bad for their [the English] character to be ruling us, as it is for our character to be ruled. I want to save my British friends from the sins of colonialism and exploitation."[53]

In response, British leaders remained carefully noncommittal about the idea of Indian independence. This did not surprise Gandhi, for he knew full well that Britain was not yet ready simply to let In-

dia go. He viewed his visit as a goodwill mission to the people of England, who he firmly believed would sooner or later accept that India must be freed. Feeling that some progress had been made, late in 1931 he sailed for home, empty-handed but hopeful.

British Parliament member Winston Churchill (pictured) disapproved of Gandhi's methods, calling them "nauseating and humiliating."

A 1931 photograph of Gandhi in London. While in London, Gandhi met with Parliament to try to persuade British leaders to grant India independence.

These hopes were soon dashed, however. When Gandhi arrived in India in December 1931, he found that a new British viceroy, Lord Willingdon, was now in charge of the country. Willingdon had proclaimed an "Emergency Powers Ordinance" to punish the Indian National Congress for its recent organization of protests on behalf of the Indian people, saying that these activities were, in effect, an effort to set up a parallel government. The imposition of martial law stripped the congress of what limited powers it had. Although the British Parliament was leaning toward giving India limited self-rule, colonial habits were hard to break; and British leaders were determined to control the process by which India became free. Gandhi tried to meet with Willingdon to appeal for a suspension of martial law, but the viceroy refused. And on January 4, 1932, Willingdon took his crackdown a step further. He declared the INC an illegal organization, confiscated its funds, and jailed its leaders, including Gandhi, all apparently in hopes of significantly slowing down the independence movement.

While in prison, Gandhi learned that the British were working to create separate political parties: one for the Hindus, one for the Muslims, and a third party for the untouchables. Clearly, this was an attempt to divide the Indian people and thereby to make any large-scale independence movement all the more difficult to mount. Under the proposed system, Hindus could only vote for Hindus; untouchables—also called *harijans*, or "children of God"— could only vote for untouchables; and Muslims could only vote for Muslims.

Gandhi detested this proposal, saying that political divisions along religious lines were both undemocratic and unethical. To him, Hinduism was a faith, not a political party. Yet he was also a realist. He knew that Hindus and Muslims were often deeply divided on many issues, so he reluctantly agreed to separate political parties for each group. Separating the untouchables from the Hindus, however, was too much for him to stomach. In his view, the untouchables needed first to be integrated into the Hindu castes so that their existence as a separate group, along with the stigma attached to it, would be erased.

After pondering how to protest the three-party system proposed by the British, Gandhi announced from his prison cell that he would fast until the Hindus and the untouchables agreed on a more unified voting arrangement. By now British officials realized the impact that Gandhi's fasts could have, so they quickly indicated willingness to change the election statutes if all parties could agree on the details. In response, Gandhi said he would fast until such an agreement was made; on September 20, 1932, he took what could well have been his last meal.

BEDSIDE NEGOTIATIONS

Almost from the beginning, this fast proved physically damaging for Gandhi. After only two days, his health was declining rapidly. To save the life of their beloved Mahatma, the leaders of the Hindu party felt they had to negotiate with the untouchables, who selected Bhimrao Ramji Ambedkar, a lawyer and social worker, as their leader. Ambedkar bargained hard with the Hindu leaders, hoping to win some political power for the untouchables, who had possessed no such power before. In the end, the negotiators agreed on a system of primaries (preliminary elections) to guarantee untouchable representation in the Hindu party without creating a separate untouchable party. Ambedkar studied the proposal meticulously and agreed to its language.

But of course, Gandhi still had to be convinced. From his bed in jail, he listened weakly as Ambedkar read the amended agreement. When some of the details did not satisfy the fasting man, more tense days of negotiation followed, during which doctors, and also Kasturbai, were summoned to Gandhi's bedside to care for him as best as they could. Finally, when the doctors predicted that Gandhi might die that day, the Hindu and untouchable negotiators worded the agreement just as he had wanted it.

The crisis was not over, however, for Gandhi refused to end his hunger strike until a representative of the British government also signed the agreement. It was Sunday in England, and no one was available in the government to sign an agreement transmitted by telegraph. Several tense hours passed, during which key leaders in England hurried to London and studied the agreement until midnight. On Monday morning, the British announced that the agreement had been signed, and on September 26, with a glass of orange juice, Gandhi finally ended his fast.

Meanwhile, as Gandhi had been fasting in the prison, far removed from the negotiations a seemingly miraculous revolution had taken place all across India. Hearing that Gandhi was willing to die to bring Hindus and untouchables together, overnight millions of Indians literally changed their ways and overthrew ancient tradition. First, a few prominent Hindu temples that had been closed to untouchables for thousands of years threw open their doors; then hundreds of other temples followed suit. Caste Hindus and untouchables began openly fraternizing in the streets, and members of the two groups began sharing food; likewise, untouchables were given access to clean well water. At the same time, thousands of organizations across India adopted resolutions promising to end all discrimination against untouchables. In Gandhi's prison cell, telegraphs informing him of these developments were stacked in a heap as tall as a man. Reporters relayed the same news to the rest of the world; and millions of people around the globe expressed wonder and/or shed tears at the realization that an entire culture had embraced positive, humanitarian change in an effort to save the life of a frail old man who refused to eat.

THE EFFECTS OF WORLD WAR II

Gandhi was pleased that so many Indians had rejected past prejudices and agreed to welcome untouchables into the mainstream of society. But for him, there was a downside to the incident. He was now more famous and widely worshiped than ever before, and he felt increasingly bothered by the constant notoriety and adoration. For this reason, early in 1934, a few months after being released from jail, he resigned from politics once again, emphasizing, as he had in the past, that he was as flawed and imperfect as any man. "I lay claim to nothing exclusively divine in me," he wrote.

> I do not claim prophetship [i.e., to be a prophet]. I am but a humble seeker after Truth and bent upon finding it. I count no sacrifice too great for the sake of seeing God face to face. The whole of my activity, whether it may be called social, political, humanitarian, or ethical, is directed to that end. And as I know that God is found more often in the lowliest of His creatures than in the high and mighty, I am struggling to reach the status of these [lowly ones]. I cannot do so without their service. Hence my passion for the service of the suppressed classes. And as I cannot render this service without entering politics, I find myself in them. Thus I am no master. I am but a struggling, erring, humble servant of India. . . . The world knows so little of how much my so-called greatness depends upon the incessant toil and drudgery of silent, devoted, able, and pure workers, men as well as women.[54]

Having retired, Gandhi appointed one of the most prominent among these devoted and able workers, Jawaharlal Nehru, to replace him as leader of the independence movement and also of the Indian National Congress, which the government had allowed to begin meeting again. For the next several years, Gandhi lived in a new community called the Sevagram Ashram, a base from which he led more marches, demonstrations, and boycotts, but he primarily concentrated on improving the welfare of the rural poor. A print of

Gandhi chose Jawaharlal Nehru (pictured) to replace him as leader of the independence movement and the Indian National Congress.

Jesus Christ hung on the mud brick wall of his one-room hut. And when visitors, who assumed he was a Hindu, asked why he had hung this picture, he replied that personal beliefs transcended formal religion. "I am a Christian, a Jew, [and] a Muslim, [as well as] a Hindu,"[55] he claimed.

Although Gandhi had formally retired from politics, ironically he remained a strong political force. When World War II began in September 1939 (with Germany's attack on Poland), without even consulting the INC the British viceroy announced that India would side with the Allied forces against Germany and its own allies. Indian leaders were so angered by this display of British arrogance that they launched a renewed, revitalized movement for full independence. Gandhi himself considered the British move so reprehensible that he came out of retirement to lead this movement, which rapidly gained force.

Faced with the probability of massive demonstrations and widespread noncooperation in one of Britain's strategically most vital colonies, the British Parliament hotly debated what to do about India. Some of the more liberal legislators favored giving India independence right away; more conservative members rejected the idea altogether; while moderates, like the highly influential member of Parliament Sir Stafford Cripps, favored a very gradual process of freeing India. Cripps, who feared a hasty withdrawal would bring chaos and upheaval to India, wrote of his concerns over too hastily granting independence to India. If that were done, he warned,

MOHANDAS GANDHI AND JAWAHARLAL NEHRU

In a History Today *article, scholar Judith Brown compares two great Indian leaders: Mohandas Gandhi and his younger ally Jawaharlal Nehru.*

"Gandhi and the younger Nehru were, of course, very different as people and also in their vision of the new India to be created as imperial rule ended. . . . [Gandhi] came from a far more provincial and less privileged background, had reached professional competence as a lawyer by strict personal discipline and a regime of self-denial and hard work. He had spent twenty formative years in South Africa, where exposure to a wide range of cultural influences and the experience of racial discrimination refined both his political skills and his religious sensibility. . . . [Nehru, by contrast,] had been brought up with everything that money could buy, educated at Harrow and Trinity College, Cambridge, and inducted with ease into the world of Indian public life by a father who was one of India's most successful and respected lawyers. With an effortless sense of superiority and no experience of hardship or personal challenge, he had no religious beliefs worth the name, and little knowledge of poor, rural India. . . . Gandhi and the somewhat aimless Jawaharlal formed a strong attachment and political partnership which was to last for almost three decades, until Gandhi's assassination in 1948. To Gandhi, Nehru was the symbol of the younger generation, the heart and touchstone of a younger India whom he needed to weld into the nationalist movement. To Nehru, Gandhi was unique in his ability to sense the mind and mood of the vast numbers of uneducated Indians, and thus essential for the forging of a broad-based nationalist movement to oust the British. But far beyond mutual need the two shared a passionate conviction that India must change radically as independence was won."

all government, which is based on the existing constitution, would immediately cease. . . . The police would cease to have any authority, courts of justice would no longer function, and there would be no laws and no order. The evil-minded could pillage the land, and disorder and crime could run riot.

. . . We make no threats, but we must assert unequivocally our duty to India, to the great minority and to the United Nations to preserve law and order until hostilities [i.e., the war with Germany] cease.[56]

Even though Cripps and others in Parliament favored a gradual rather than sudden loosening of Britain's hold on India, Winston Churchill, now Britain's prime minister, staunchly opposed the whole idea of Indian independence. "I have not become the King's First Minister in order to preside at the liquidation of the British Empire,"[57] he said. Such statements from the highest levels of British government made it abundantly clear to disappointed Indians of all social classes that the dream of an independent India would have to wait still longer to be fulfilled.

Chapter

6 Independence at Last

In March 1941 the British promised to grant India its independence after the war was over. Despite this promise, Gandhi, now out of retirement, still refused to support the British war effort. He called the British promise a postdated check. In response, the Indian National Congress passed a "Quit India" resolution, calling for mass nonviolent protests. "We shall either free India or die in the attempt; we shall not live to see the perpetuation of our slavery,"[58] the resolution stated.

Gandhi announced that if the British did not leave, the Quit India movement would launch the largest ever civil disobedience campaign. But he never started any new campaign without making one last attempt to negotiate a settlement. To this end, he asked for an immediate meeting with Lord Linlithgow, the latest British viceroy of India. Under British orders not to negotiate and to do something to discourage the protesters, the viceroy immediately jailed Gandhi and other top Indian leaders. Incarcerated once again, Gandhi was isolated from the press and kept from reading the news. He could not communicate with the Indian people at all, and since he was the only public figure who could effectively orchestrate large-scale demonstrations against the British, the nonviolent component of the independence movement was effectively stalled.

Even without Gandhi, the Quit India campaign went on, however, and over the next few months nearly one hundred thousand Indian protesters joined Gandhi in jail. Soon India exploded in violence. Buildings were set on fire, train tracks were ripped out, British officials were assaulted and killed, and underground movements sprang up everywhere. The viceroy unfairly blamed Gandhi, who, because he did not condone the violence, was actually beside himself with grief and frustration. To protest this false accusation that he was behind the violence, he decided to undertake a three-week fast. Well aware of the effectiveness of past Gandhian fasts, the viceroy offered to release him before the fast began, but the Mahatma refused and replied that he was not fasting to win his release but rather to protest his innocence.

Gandhi finished his twenty-one-day fast but remained in prison. It was during this stay in jail that he learned to his distress that his wife was gravely ill. Confined to prison herself (because of her

Gandhi's wife Kasturbai died in prison on February 22, 1944. Some critics asserted that her life might have been prolonged if Gandhi had allowed doctors to treat her bronchitis with antibiotics.

her the use of antibiotics might have hastened Kasturbai's death, but he showed no remorse about his decision, saying it was based on both his and his wife's deeply held religious convictions. Kasturbai's death was God's will, he believed, so he must accept it.

Not long after Kasturbai's death, Gandhi himself grew seriously ill. He developed a severe case of malaria, and within a few weeks his doctors said he was near death. British officials decided that it might further damage their image with the Indian populace if Gandhi died in their prison, so on May 6, 1944, they released him; however, to their great surprise, he managed once again to recover and was soon able to resume his humanitarian and political activities.

NEGOTIATING INDEPENDENCE

Gandhi was released from prison at about the time that the Indian struggle for independence was entering its final stages. In 1945, with World War II at an end, the goal of that struggle—a free nation of India—seemed finally to loom in sight. However, a serious stumbling block still remained—namely, disagreements and conflict between Indian Hindus and Muslims. The leader of the Muslims, Mohammed Ali Jinnah, feared that Muslims would have no effective political power in a Hindu-dominated India. He proposed that six Indian provinces—Punjab, Sind, Bengal, Baluchistan, Assam, and the North-West Frontier—become the separate Muslim nation of Pakistan. Not surprisingly,

protest activities), Kasturbai, now seventy-four, had contracted chronic bronchitis. Gandhi, who was opposed to any medical treatment that involved puncturing the body with a foreign object, refused to allow the use of antibiotics to treat her illness; she died in her cell on February 22, 1944. Some of Gandhi's critics have suggested that his denying

Gandhi strongly objected to the prospect of such a partition, or division, of the country. The six provinces Jinnah specified made up nearly a fourth of India's territory, and the division would leave a huge minority of 47 million non-Muslims in Pakistan. Moreover, some 20 million Muslims would still be living in India. Gandhi feared for the safety of these minorities following partition and was determined to keep India united.

In 1946 some members of the British Cabinet arrived in India to determine how to arrange for a smooth transition to an independent India. These officials were naturally concerned about the ongoing differences between the country's Hindu and Muslim factions and worked to try to resolve these differences so that Indian independence could indeed become a reality as soon as possible. The British prime minister, Clement Attlee, described the mission in a speech:

> "My colleagues are going to India with the intention of using their utmost endeavors to help her to attain her freedom as speedily and fully as possible. What form of Government is to replace the present regime is for India to decide; but our desire is to help [India] to set up forthwith the machinery for making that decision."[59]

The British soon found, however, that the differences between Hindus and Muslims were more pronounced than they had expected; and because the two groups could not agree on key issues, British leaders felt it was their duty to put forward an independence plan of their own.

In fact, the British Labor Party, which had recently come to power in Britain, now firmly favored "quitting" India, regardless of the friction between Indian Hindus and Muslims. Labor Party leaders proposed the formation of an Indian Cabinet that represented all of the parties involved; but when the Hindu and Muslim parties could not agree on the structure of such a Cabinet, the British directed Gandhi's protégé, Nehru, who had been chosen to lead an interim government, to appoint eleven Cabinet ministers.

NEHRU NAMED PRIME MINISTER

Nehru, who was to be the president of the Indian Cabinet, tried to accommodate a variety of views in that ruling body. To that end he named five Hindus, one untouchable, two Muslims, and three representatives of much smaller religious minorities (Sikh, Christian, and Parsi) to the Cabinet seats. But this selection angered Jinnah, who wanted more Muslim representation. He declared August 16, 1946, to be "Direct Action Day." On that day, gangs of armed Muslims took to the streets of Calcutta to attack Hindus, and Hindu reprisals were equally vicious. By the time order was finally restored, more than five thousand Indians were dead and fifteen thousand were wounded.

A few weeks after the riots, the British named Nehru as the prime minister of India. Jinnah immediately pronounced this a Muslim day of mourning, and new riots broke out in Bombay, Punjab, Bihar, and Bengal. With the country seemingly on

Prime Minister Jawaharlal Nehru (left) and his mentor Gandhi. To resolve India's religious turmoil, Nehru appointed a diverse Cabinet, but his efforts were to no avail and the violence continued.

the brink of religious civil war, in desperation Nehru appointed five Muslim Cabinet members; but the new appointees announced that they did not recognize Nehru's government as legitimate and refused to participate. India was now firmly divided along religious lines, and the violence continued. Even in remote villages, Hindus and Muslims beat, raped, and murdered one another.

As might be expected, Gandhi was deeply saddened that Indians were killing one another instead of celebrating their newfound freedom. "If India makes violence her creed, and I have survived," he wrote,

> I would not care to live in India. She will cease to evoke any pride in me. My patriotism is subservient to my religion. I cling to India like a child to its mother's breast because I feel that she gives me the spiritual nourishment I need. She has the environment that responds to my highest aspirations. When that faith is gone, I shall feel like an orphan without hope of ever finding a guardian.[60]

*Gandhi travels from village to village in India, spreading his message of
nonviolence. Gandhi hoped that his presence would encourage Hindus and
Muslims to cease hostilities.*

Hoping that his very presence would help
save lives and restore the peace, Gandhi began to tour the ravaged country. Along the
way, thousands of people besieged his
train, seeking his blessing. He traveled to
Calcutta, now a city full of gutted buildings
and garbage-strewn streets; and on each
day that he spent in this and other cities, he
spoke out against the violence, hoping that
his words would pacify the angry mobs.
These efforts did pay off in the province of
Bengal, where Gandhi's presence brought

calm and order. But he could not be everywhere at once, and elsewhere the situation
raced out of control, with violent acts in
one city triggering violent reprisals in another. Ever the optimist, Gandhi remained
hopeful that these disorders would soon
subside, that Hindus and Muslims would
find some way to return to peaceful coexis-
tence in a unified nation. The reality, however, was that many on both sides were
sharpening the knives with which they
would soon carve up India.

The Partitioning of India

As time went on, the British increasingly realized that India could not avoid some kind of violent upheaval or partitioning, and leaders in London decided that it was best for Britain to avoid getting involved in the troubles ahead. In June 1947, therefore, the British announced that, despite whether a formal independence agreement

---

Gandhi's Mixed Legacy in India

In the October 29, 1998, issue of the Christian Science Monitor *author Robert Marquand discusses Gandhi's legacy for India and the world. Marquand notes that Gandhi's face appears on coins, stamps, and billboards, yet the unity Gandhi sought is hard to find in India today.*

"Gandhi provided the glue that unified India, a nation formerly divided into more than 500 princely fiefdoms. His social genius and homespun ways, simple truths of love and compassion, marches and fasts against violence fired the people's imagination. His nonviolent opposition to British rule liberated India and helped topple colonial empires the world over. . . . Even in India no politician dares openly challenge the memory of the Mahatma. His face appears on the 10-rupee note, the most common currency in India. Schoolchildren learn [Indian poet] Rabindranath Tagore's famous lines that Gandhi 'stopped at the thresholds of the huts of the thousands of the dispossessed. . . . When love came to the door of India, that door was opened wide. . . . At Gandhi's call India blossomed forth to new greatness.'. . .[Today] in politics, the Congress Party Gandhi helped found is out of power and in disarray; members argue over who is most corrupt. The ideal of a unified India has never been weaker. . . . Many Indians have lost the tone of Gandhi's life, according to Amrut Modi of the Gandhi Ashram in Ahmedabad. . . . [Yet] Gandhi may have the last word. The most effective and organized parts of Indian society today, and the most thriving, are the non-governmental organizations that have spread out across Indian villages. Most are consciously patterned on Gandhian views. Volunteer and nonprofit groups that deal with water, birth control, human rights for women and the lower castes, peace groups, child care, wise land use, the environment, remedial education, agricultural training . . . all pick up Gandhian values and are proliferating through the countryside."

had been reached, they were quitting India in August. Lord Mountbatten, the last viceroy of India, made one final attempt to reconcile the differences between the Hindus and the Muslims. Realizing that partition was now almost a certainty, he persuaded the Indian National Congress to agree to divide India up in a manner that did not strand large populations of Hindus in Pakistan. Disregarding Gandhi's objections to the very idea of partition, the congress and Jinnah approved the plan; on August 15 Britain granted India independence and the status of a nation in the British Commonwealth.

Millions of Indians rejoiced at achieving true nationhood at last. But Gandhi refused to celebrate India's independence because he feared that the partition that resulted in the creation of India and Pakistan would only deepen hostilities between Hindus and Muslims and lead to increased violence. And this assessment proved correct. Over the next several

Lord and Lady Mountbatten, the last viceroy and vicereine of India, just prior to their departure from India.

Gandhi appeals to Hindus and Muslims to end the factional strife ravaging India. The violence was so extreme that sometimes entire villages were massacred.

months, rioting, burning, looting, beatings, killings, and seizures of property became commonplace all over India. Brutal massacres wiped out entire families and even whole villages. Some 15 million Indians were uprooted as displaced Muslim refugees streamed toward Pakistan and Hindu refugees marched toward India. So massive were their numbers that one convoy of refugees stretched over fifty-seven miles. The sick and decrepit collapsed along the roads and vultures circled overhead; cholera, smallpox, and other diseases ravaged the survivors. Yet in the midst of all this chaos, exhaustion, and suffering, when columns of Muslims met columns of Hindus, the two groups still somehow found the strength to attack each other.

The city of Delhi was particularly hard hit by violence. And into this dangerous cauldron of hatred, fighting, and looting Gandhi calmly entered on foot. Respect and reverence for him was still strong, for incredibly, as he strode toward angry crowds of Hindus and Muslims assaulting one another with sticks and rocks, they stopped fighting and parted to let him through. He

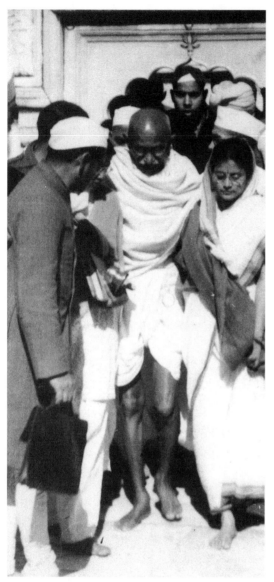

This photo, taken on January 27, 1948, is believed to be the last photo of Gandhi alive. He was assassinated four days later.

so to reach the hearts and minds of his countrymen on a wider scale, he decided that he must fast again. In doing so, he appealed to the consciences of all Indians— Hindus, Muslims, and those of other faiths as well. Only if and when he saw sincere, detailed plans to curb the violence, he said, would he eat again.

On January 13, 1948, Gandhi began his fast. Five days later, on January 18, about one hundred representatives of the Hindu, Muslim, Sikh, Christian, Jewish, and other religions practiced in the country presented themselves at his bedside. They had brought with them a document promising peace and property rights for all faiths throughout India. When the Mahatma asked whether his visitors were trying to deceive him just to save his life, those present solemnly pledged their commitment to peace. Hearing this, Gandhi became convinced that he could better serve the cause of peace by living and ended his fast.

GANDHI'S LAST DAY

In the days following Gandhi's agreement to conclude his fast, the violence between Hindus and Muslims largely subsided. A small group of radical Hindus, however, did not want any kind of peace with Muslims, deeply resented the division of India, and advocated attacking Pakistan in order to restore India to its former borders. Although Gandhi had originally opposed partition, the radicals felt that Gandhi opposed their ideals since he had, in the interests of peace and harmony, decided to accept partition as

then strolled among the former rioters, smiling and offering them his blessings. Wherever Gandhi went, the results were the same: Anger and fighting quickly subsided. But once again, he could not be everywhere;

inevitable. In the eyes of the radicals, the success of his influential campaigns of nonviolence made him a major obstacle to a reunified India under Hindu control. It was high time, they decided, to get rid of this obstacle.

Gandhi himself made it fairly simple for the radicals to carry out their plan; this was because he was a giving, open person who always made himself accessible to anyone who wanted to see him. Security around him was nearly nonexistent; he had no personal guards, and the police were usually lax about providing him with protection.

On Gandhi's last day of life, Friday, January 30, 1948, the now seventy-eight-year-old man rose from his pallet on the floor of the glassed-in porch where he slept and woke his companions, who

---

GANDHISM IN INDIA TODAY

An August 28, 1998, article in the Economist *magazine reports that religious division, caste restrictions, Hindu nationalism, and conflicts with Pakistan still plague India and that the path of nonviolence is no longer taken seriously by people in leadership positions.*

"[Noted historian] Arnold Toynbee, wrote, 'The only salvation for mankind is the Indian way.' His faith in India was once as commonplace as his despair over the superpowers. Unlike the United States and the Soviet Union, India was founded by a genuine saint: Mohandas Gandhi, who broke the British empire with hunger strikes and a spinning wheel, and Jawaharlal Nehru, the first Prime minister, made democracy, socialism, religious tolerance and non-alignment the pillars of the new state. Westerners from E. M. Forester to the Beatles trooped to India for decades in search of virtues they could not find at home. While Gandhi and Nehru were alive, it seemed possible to believe that India would be great because she was good. Alas, the dream of greatness proved hardier than dedication to goodness. The bloody partition that carved Islamic Pakistan out of Hindu-dominated India was the first and greatest insult to Nehru's sect-blind creed. Over the next half-century, the affronts to that and other ideals hardly ceased. Nehru's daughter, Indira Gandhi, temporarily assumed dictatorial powers in 1975. It was she who injected into mainstream politics the notion that 'Indian' and 'Hindu' were synonyms, an idea that animates the current ruling party, the Bharatiya Janata Party."

included his young grandnieces Manu and Abha. He brushed his teeth. Then the group said prayers from the *Bhagavad Gita*, and when they finished the girls helped him walk inside and covered his bare legs with a blanket. That afternoon, Gandhi rested outside with a peasant's bamboo hat shading his face. A journalist, a French photographer, a professor, some groups of blind and homeless refugees, and a few Muslim leaders came to discuss pressing issues of the day with him. At 4:00 P.M., two prominent Indian politicians came and told Manu that they wished to see Gandhi. When she asked him if he wanted to see them, he replied, "Tell them that I will, but only after the prayer meeting, and that too if I am still living."[61] At 5:00 P.M., prayer time, he walked slowly outside, leaning on two walking sticks and also aided by Manu and Abha. It was a two-hundred-yard walk to the prayer platform, and just two yards before reaching the platform's stairs, Gandhi turned and pressed his palms together, a sign of greeting to the crowd of several hundred people that parted for him. In that moment, a young Hindu man named Nathuram Godse pushed through the crowd and bowed to Gandhi. Unbeknownst to all present, his own joined palms hid a small black pistol. Gandhi blessed Godse, then motioned him away. But Godse rushed forward, pushed Manu aside, and shot Gandhi three times in the abdomen and chest. As the third bullet punctured his body, Gandhi gasped. "Oh God, oh God,"[62] he managed to say, then sank to the ground and died. As the crowd panicked, some nearby policemen who had heard the shots rushed over and struggled to maintain order. Mahatma Gandhi's two grandnieces cradled him in their laps as his face paled and blood slowly stained his white shawl a bright crimson.

THE WORLD GRIEVES

Gandhi's death had the effect of bringing temporary peace to India as Hindus, Muslims, and Indians of other faiths and walks of life joined in mourning him. The radical Hindu conspirators who had planned his assassination had believed that once he was out of the way any attempts to maintain peace between Hindus and Muslims would fail and that India would attack Pakistan. But what actually happened was far different. First, the people of both India and Pakistan honored his memory by grieving him in peace. His funeral procession was attended by over a million Indians and Pakistanis, a majority of whom were so stricken with anguish and grief that thereafter they walked about in a stupor for days, weeks, and even months. And in a final tribute to Gandhi's commitment to peace, many Hindus and Muslims tried to put aside their hatred of one another and to begin learning to live in peace.

Meanwhile, many millions of other people worldwide sadly noted Gandhi's passing. Notables from around the globe, including physicist Albert Einstein, American general Douglas MacArthur, Soviet leader Andrey Gromyko, the Catholic pope, the Dalai Lama of Tibet, Britain's archbishop of Canterbury, England's king George V, U.S. president Harry Truman, and Chinese

A souvenir hunter scoops ashes from Gandhi's funeral pyre in New Delhi. Over a million people attended his funeral procession, and millions more mourned his death worldwide.

leader Chiang Kai-shek, praised and eulogized Gandhi. And the United Nations lowered its flag to half-mast as a sign of respect.

Out of all the tributes to Gandhi's memory in the months following his death, two of the most touching, and perhaps the ones that best captured his importance as a humanitarian reformer, great leader, and inspiration to later generations, were those voiced by his longtime friend Jawaharlal Nehru and the renowned scientist Albert Einstein. "The light has gone out of our lives," said Nehru,

and there is darkness everywhere . . . and yet . . . the light that shone in this country [during Gandhi's lifetime] was no ordinary light. The light that has illumined this country for these many years will illumine [it] for many more years, and a thousand years later that light will still be seen in this country, and the world will see it and it will give solace to innumerable hearts.[63]

Einstein added, simply and appropriately, "Generations to come, it may be, will scarce believe that such a one as this ever in flesh and blood walked upon this earth."[64]

Epilogue

Gandhi's Legacy

At the dawn of the twenty-first century, Gandhi's legacy for India and the world is still being written. The nation he helped to create through peaceful means is still trying, with only mixed results, to live in harmony with its neighbor Pakistan. In the 1970s, 1980s, and 1990s, the two nations had a number of serious disagreements; and both have recently developed and tested nuclear weapons. These developments continue to worry most of the other nations in the world, who fear that a war between the Indians and Pakistanis might escalate into a broader conflict that would draw in many other countries.

Within India itself, though caste restrictions eased and untouchables became full citizens, religious, caste, and class divisions remain firmly in place today, more than fifty years after Gandhi's death. He did manage to establish a handful of small industries that still produce clothing, food, and crafts; however, for the most part large manufacturing companies and business corporations now dominate the Indian economy, as they do the economies of Western industrialized nations like the United States and India's old master, Britain. In addition, although more Indians have managed to climb into the middle class than in Gandhi's day, three-quarters of all Indians remain locked in rural poverty.

Still, Mohandas Gandhi's lasting legacy to the world is concerned with much more than reaching specific political, social, and ethical goals. His unique gift was demonstrating that one need not be rich and powerful to effect real, positive change in the world. By example, he showed that human beings are capable of courage, unity, and self-sacrifice; that it is possible to fight violence with nonviolence and win; and that deeply divided people can bridge great divides. Respect for others is within every person's grasp, he taught, and being a good human being does not depend on wealth, genius, good looks, skin color, or other superficial traits.

Since Gandhi's death, these messages have inspired movements around the world against violence, racism, and colonialism. In 1968, for example, Czech civilians nonviolently held Soviet armed forces at bay. And in the United States, also in the 1960s, Martin Luther King Jr. and other U.S. civil rights activists applied Gandhi's principles of nonviolent struggle to their

GANDHI AND KING—LIVING AND DYING FOR NONVIOLENCE

In March 1998, Billy O. Wireman, president of Queens College in Charlotte, North Carolina, spoke at the Martin Luther King Day celebration. Wireman examined how Gandhi's life and work influenced King, the great American civil rights crusader. His speech is reprinted in the March 1, 1998, issue of Vital Speeches of the Day.

"As we pause tonight . . . to reflect on the life and work of Dr. King, I want us to think together about the forces that shaped his values. . . . In his childhood, I asked [his father], Martin Luther King Sr., 'did you see any evidence that your son, Martin, would achieve such distinction?' 'Heavens no,' 'Daddy' King responded. 'He drifted until he connected Christianity to Gandhi.' For seventy-five years—from 1893 when Gandhi went to South Africa as a twenty-three-year-old London-educated barrister, to 1968, when King was murdered in Memphis—these two inspired men fought hate with love, and greed with openhandedness. . . . Having lived, and died, for nonviolence, it is puzzling why many today consider Gandhi and King irrelevant. In a world awash with ethnic violence, what could be more relevant than King's call for people to 'not be judged by the color of their skin, but by the content of their character.' What could be more timely than King's . . . tenet that individuals must reach deep into their souls and with their own pens . . . write their own Emancipation Proclamations? And who can deny Gandhi's impeccable logic [that violence begets only more violence, creating a violent cycle, and that a commitment to nonviolence breaks that cycle]? An eye for an eye leads to blindness by both parties. Like reformers everywhere, these men were scorned for their beliefs. . . . In the end, they were destroyed by the very passions they unleashed. However, their efforts will not have been in vain [for the world as a whole will one day come around to their way of thinking]."

A portrait of Gandhi, signed by the inspirational leader.

own battles for racial equality. Reverend King, like Gandhi, believed that violence begets only more violence rather than peace and understanding, which should be the goal of all reasonable, decent people. "Jesus gave us the strategy of nonviolence and Gandhi gave us the tactic," King said. "We may ignore Gandhi at our own risk."[65]

Notes

Introduction: The Father of Nonviolence

1. M. K. Gandhi, *Selected Writings*, ed. Ronald Duncan. New York: Harper, 1971, pp. 65–66.

2. Gandhi, *Selected Writings*, p. 49.

3. Quoted in Louis Fischer, *The Life of Mahatma Gandhi*. New York: Collier Books, 1950, p. 17.

Chapter 1: Coming of Age in British India and London

4. M. K. Gandhi, *Autobiography: The Story of My Experiments with Truth*, trans. Mahadev Desai. New York: Dover, 1983, pp. 29–30.

5. Gandhi, *Autobiography*, p. 2.

6. Gandhi, *Autobiography*, p. 4.

7. Gandhi, *Autobiography*, pp. 3–4.

8. Gandhi, *Autobiography*, p. 24.

9. Quoted in Homer A. Jack, *The Gandhi Reader*. Bloomington: Indiana University Press, 1956, p. 24.

10. Gandhi, *Autobiography*, pp. 36–37.

11. Gandhi, *Autobiography*, p. 60.

12. Gandhi, *Autobiography*, pp. 70–71.

Chapter 2: From India to the Colonies of South Africa

13. Gandhi, *Autobiography*, p. 75.

14. Gandhi, *Autobiography*, pp. 73, 81–82.

15. Gandhi, *Autobiography*, pp. 78–79.

16. Gandhi, *Autobiography*, p. 79.

17. Quoted in Taya Zinkin, *The Story of Gandhi*. New York: Criterion Books, 1965, p. 62.

18. Quoted in Zinkin, *The Story of Gandhi*, p. 63.

Chapter 3: Gandhi's Stormy Return to South Africa

19. Quoted in Zinkin, *The Story of Gandhi*, p. 76.

20. Ashe, *Gandhi*, p. 72.

21. Quoted in Geoffrey Ashe, *Gandhi*. New York: Stein and Day, 1968, p.66.

22. M. K. Gandhi, *Satyagraha in South Africa*. Ahmadabad, India: Navajivan, 1928, p. 88.

23. Gandhi, *Autobiography*, p. 281.

24. Gandhi, *Autobiography*, p. 281.

25. Quoted in Ashe, *Gandhi*, p. 98.

26. Gandhi, *Satyagraga in South Africa*, p. 177.

27. M. K. Gandhi, *The Collected Works of Mahatma Gandhi*, vol. 12. Delhi: Government of India, Ministry of Information and Broadcasting, 1958, pp. 507–508.

28. Quoted in Fischer, *The Life of Mahatma Gandhi*, p. 65.

29. Quoted in Penderal Moon, *Gandhi and Modern India*. New York: Norton, 1969, p. 71.

30. Quoted in Ashe, *Gandhi*, p. 125.

Chapter 4: The Mahatma Comes Home

31. Quoted in Louis Fischer, *Gandhi: His Life and Message for the World*. New York: New American Library, 1954, p. 54.

32. Quoted in Fischer, *Gandhi*, p. 50.

33. Quoted in Robert Payne, *The Life and Death of Mahatma Gandhi*. New York: Konecky and Konecky, 1969, p. 296.

34. Gandhi, *Selected Writings*, pp. 48–49.

35. Quoted in Jack, *The Gandhi Reader*, p. 104.

36. Quoted in Moon, *Gandhi and Modern India*, p. 86.

37. Quoted in Fischer, *Gandhi*, p. 82.

38. Quoted in Fischer, *The Life of Mahatma Gandhi*, p. 130.

39. Quoted in R. K. Prabhu and U. R. Rao, *The Mind of Mahatma Gandhi*. Ahmadabad, India: Navjivan, 1998, p. 23.

40. Quoted in Fischer, *Gandhi*, p. 60.

41. Quoted in Prabhu and Rao, *The Mind of Mahatma Gandhi*, p. 82.

42. Quoted in Prabhu and Rao, *The Mind of Mahatma Gandhi*, p. 114.

43. Quoted in Prabhu and Rao, *The Mind of Mahatma Gandhi*, p. 172.

44. Quoted in Prabhu and Rao, *The Mind of Mahatma Gandhi*, p. 110.

45. Quoted in Fischer, *Gandhi*, p. 72.

46. Quoted in Fischer, *The Life of Mahatma Gandhi*, p. 232.

47. Quoted in Fischer, *The Life of Mahatma Gandhi*, p. 74.

48. Quoted in Fischer, *The Life of Mahatma Gandhi*, p. 236.

Chapter 5: The Road to Independence

49. Quoted in Fischer, *The Life of Mahatma Gandhi*, p. 220.

50. Quoted in Zinkin, *The Story of Gandhi*, p. 154.

51. Quoted in Zinkin, *The Story of Gandhi*, p. 155.

52. Quoted in Fischer, *The Life of Mahatma Gandhi*, p. 103.

53. Quoted in Zinkin, *The Story of Gandhi*, p. 165.

54. Quoted in Fischer, *Gandhi*, p. 82.

55. Quoted in Zinkin, *The Story of Gandhi*, p. 171.

56. Quoted in *London Times*, "Statement on India," August 6, 1942.

57. Quoted in Fischer, *Gandhi*, p. 138.

Chapter 6: Independence at Last

58. Quoted in Moon, *Gandhi and Modern India*, p. 234.

59. Quoted in Brian McArthur, ed., *The Penguin Book of Twentieth Century Speeches*. London: Penguin Viking, 1992, pp. 234–35.

60. Quoted in Prabhu and Rao, *The Mind of Mahatma Gandhi*, p. 222.

61. Quoted in Jack, *The Gandhi Reader*, p. 475.

62. Quoted in Fischer, *The Life of Mahatma Gandhi*, p. 504.

63. Quoted in Louis Fischer, *The Essential Gandhi*. New York: Random House, 1962, pp. 368–69.

64. Quoted in Fischer, *The Essential Gandhi*, p. 369.

Epilogue: Gandhi's Legacy

65. Quoted in Mahatma Gandhi, Physicians for Global Survival, Canada. www.pgs.ca/pages/mem/gandhi.htm.

Glossary

apartheid: The official South African policy of political, legal, and economic discrimination against nonwhites.

ashram: A religious community, school, or retreat.

Bhagavad Gita: A Hindu religious text written in Sanskrit, an ancient language of India.

bramacharya: Self-control exercised through abstinence from sexual relations.

caste system: A system of social organization that divides the population into fixed classes; membership is determined at birth.

civil disobedience: The deliberate breaking of unjust laws with the aim of protesting injustices.

guru: In the Hindu religion, a spiritual teacher or mentor who is close to God.

Parsi: An Indian religion derived from the followers of the ancient prophet Zoroaster, who came to India fleeing Persian Muslims.

satyagraha: Gandhi's name for his movement of nonviolent resistance. Loosely translated, it means "force of truth and love."

suttee: An ancient Indian tradition of burning widows alive on their husbands' funeral pyres.

untouchables: A class of Indians without caste privileges, who were confined to the lowest jobs and living quarters.

viceroy: The highest ranking British officer in British-controlled India and a representative of the king of England.

For Further Reading

Books

Catherine Bush, *Gandhi*. New York: Chelsea House, 1985. A readable general synopsis of Gandhi's life and accomplishments, aimed at junior high school readers.

Narayan Desai, *Gandhi Through a Child's Eyes: An Intimate Memoir*. Santa Fe: Ocean Tree Books, 1992. The son of Mohandas Gandhi's personal secretary describes growing up in that household and gives a portrait of the Indian leader at home during the years 1924 to 1942.

Catherine O. Peare, *Mahatma Gandhi: Father of Nonviolence*. New York: Hawthorne Books, 1969. A spirited, easy-to-read version of Gandhi's life, aimed at young readers.

John B. Severance, *Gandhi: Great Soul*. New York: Houghton Mifflin, 1997. An in-depth survey of Gandhi's life and political activities illustrated with black-and-white period photographs.

Websites

Gandhian Charitable Institution (www.mkgandhisarvodaya.org/index.html). A collection of information about Gandhi's life and philosophy.

The Gandhi Virtual Ashram (www.nuvs.com/ashram/index.html). A general collection of information about and photos of Gandhi.

The Indian History Sourcebook (www.fordham.edu/halsall). Contains an overview of important modern historical events, including India's fight for independence.

Mahatma Gandhi Album (www.engaged-page.com/gandhi.html). Contains information about Gandhi's lifestyle and his ideas about vegetarianism.

Mahatma Gandhi Research and Media Service (www.gandhiserve.com/). Contains many of Gandhi's writings, recordings of his voice, photos, and other material.

Movie

Gandhi (1982). Directed by Richard Attenborough; written by John Briley. This long, stately, beautifully acted and photographed film about Gandhi's adult exploits won many Oscars and other awards and is highly recommended for all.

Works Consulted

Books

Geoffrey Ashe, *Gandhi*. New York: Stein and Day, 1968. This insightful biography of Gandhi examines and analyzes his life within the context of his time.

Shakti Batra, *The Quintessence of Gandhi: In His Own Words*. New Delhi, India: Madhu Muskan, 1984. A large and well-organized collection of Gandhi quotes and writings on diverse subjects.

Judith Brown, *A Prisoner of Hope*. New Haven, CT: Yale University Press, 1991. This work details Gandhi's fascinating and complex life. An important source.

Yogesh Chada, *Gandhi: A Life*. New York: John Wiley and Sons, 1998. The first major Gandhi biography in over twenty years offers a gripping narrative that is balanced, fair, and inspirational.

Erik H. Erikson, *Gandhi's Truth on the Origins of Militant Nonviolence*. New York: Norton, 1969. Examines how Gandhi influenced reform movements and revolutions in the twentieth century.

Louis Fischer, *The Essential Gandhi*. New York: Random House, 1962. An anthology of Gandhi's writings taken from newspapers, magazines, letters, speeches, and his autobiography.

———, *Gandhi: His Life and Message for the World*. New York: New American Library, 1954. An accessible and thoughtful work that discusses the relevance of Gandhism to the entire world. The book is written by one of Gandhi's most prolific biographers.

———, *The Life of Mahatma Gandhi*. New York: Collier Books, 1950. This first biography of Gandhi by Fischer has a narrative flow that makes Gandhi's life come vividly alive.

Arun Gandhi et al., *The Forgotten Woman: The Untold Story of Kasturbai Gandhi, Wife of Mahatma Gandhi*. Huntsville, AK: Ozark Mountain, 1998. A biography of Gandhi's wife, by her grandson, that sheds important light on a remarkable woman.

M. K. Gandhi, *Autobiography: The Story of My Experiments with Truth*. Trans. Mahadev Desai. New York: Dover, 1983. A fascinating account that relays Gandhi's thoughts at critical moments in his life.

———, *The Collected Works of Mahatma Gandhi*. Vol. 12. Delhi: Government of India, Ministry of Information and Broadcasting, 1958. A comprehensive selection of Gandhi's writings.

———, *"Hind Swaraj" and Other Writings*. Ed. A. J. Parel. New York: Cambridge University Press, 1997. Mahatma Gandhi's original 1910 edition of this work, favoring "home rule" for India.

It also includes Gandhi's correspondence with Tolstoy, Nehru, and other national and world leaders.

————, *Satyagraha in South Africa*. Ahmadabad, India: Navajivan, 1928. The story of Gandhi's efforts to fight for the civil rights of the Indian community in South Africa, as told by Gandhi himself.

————, *Selected Writings*. Ed. Ronald Duncan. New York: Harper, 1971. A useful collection of excerpts from Gandhi's many works.

James Heitzman and Robert L. Worden, eds., *India: A Country Study*. Washington, DC: Library of Congress, 1996. A huge, detailed, and up-to-date compendium of geographical, historical, political, social, and other facts about India.

Francis G. Hutchins, *India's Revolution: Gandhi and the Quit India Movement*. Cambridge, MA: Harvard University Press, 1973. Provides an overview of India's independence movement and Gandhi's role in it.

Homer A. Jack, *The Gandhi Reader*. Bloomington: Indiana University Press, 1956. A collection of writings by and about Gandhi.

Brian McArthur, ed., *The Penguin Book of Twentieth Century Speeches*. London: Penguin Viking, 1992. Contains hundreds of public speeches by noted officials and other public personalities who have helped to shape the course of the century's history.

Ved Mehta, *Mahatma Gandhi and His Apostles*. New York: Viking, 1977. An attempt to provide a less worshipful profile of Gandhi, laying bare his flaws and failures as well as his admirable qualities and successes.

Penderel Moon, *Gandhi and Modern India*. New York: Norton, 1969. A commendable account of Gandhi's nonviolent protests and his impact on modern India and the world.

Dadabhai Naoroji, *Essays, Speeches, Addresses, and Writings*. Bombay: Caxton Printing Works, 1887. Historical material that touches on aspects of Indian politics and government.

Robert Payne, *The Life and Death of Mahatma Gandhi*. New York: Konecky and Konecky, 1969. A thorough treatment of Gandhi that includes material absent in other biographies, including a description of the assassin's trial.

R. K. Prabhu and U. R. Rao, *The Mind of Mahatma Gandhi*. Ahmadabad, India: Navjivan, 1998. A large encyclopedic collection of thoughts and sayings of M. K. Gandhi.

Percival Spear, *India: A Modern History*. Ann Arbor: University of Michigan Press, 1961. An excellent overview of Indian history up to the midpoint of the twentieth century, this provides a useful context for understanding the political and social problems faced by that country and how Gandhi's efforts fit into the bigger picture.

Maureen Swan, *The South African Experience*. Johannesburg, South Africa: Ravan, 1985. This book provides some interesting insights into Gandhi as a practicing lawyer and practical politician. The reader gets a clearer picture of Gandhi's compromises.

Taya Zinkin, *The Story of Gandhi.* New York: Criterion Books, 1965. A short, breezy biography focusing on highlights of Gandhi's life.

Periodicals

Atlantic Monthly, "British India," November 1857.

Surendra Bhana, "The Tolstoy Farm: Gandhi's Experiment in Cooperative Commonwealth," *South African Historical Journal*, November 1975.

Economist, "Deconsecrating Gandhi," August 28, 1998.

London Times, "Statement on India," August 6, 1942.

Robert Marquand, "Can India Stay True to Gandhi?" *Christian Science Monitor*, October 29, 1998.

Ralph Summy, "Nonviolence Around the World: The Triumph of Gandhi," *Social Alternatives*, April 1997.

U.S. Department of State Annual Report on International Religious Freedom for 1999: India. Washington, DC: Bureau for Democracy, Human Rights, and Labor, September 9, 1999.

Billy O. Wireman, "God's Co-Workers for Justice," *Vital Speeches of the Day*, March 1, 1998.

Internet Sources

Andre Brink, "Mahatma Gandhi Today," 1970, African National Congress homepage. www.anc.org.za/ancdocs/history/people/gandhi/brink.html.

Judith Brown, "Nehru and Gandhi," *History Today*, September 1997. www.historytoday.com.

International Fellowship of Reconciliation, "Appeal of the Nobel Peace Prize Laureates for a Culture of Nonviolence." www.ifor.org/.

———, "Gandhiji's Writings." www.itihaas.com/modern/gandhi-writing.html.

Mark Lindley, "How Gandhi Came to Believe Caste Must Be Dismantled by Intermarriage," European Vegetarian Union. www.ivu.org/evu/news981/gandhi2.html.

Mahatma Gandhi, Physicians for Global Survival, Canada. www.pgs.ca/pages/mem/gandhi.htm.

Nelson Mandela, "Speech at Conferral of Freedom of Pietermaritzburg on Mahatma Gandhi," April 25, 1997, African National Congress homepage. www.anc.org.za/ancdocs/history/mandela/1997/sp970425a.html.

Leah Renold, "Gandhi: Patron Saint of the Industrialist," 1994, Asian Studies Network Information Center Website, University of Texas. http://asnic.utexax.edu/asnic/sagar/spring.1994/leah.renold.art.html.

Henry David Thoreau, "Resistance to Civil Government or Civil Disobedience," American Transcendentalism Web, Virginia Commonwealth University. www.vcu.edu/engweb/transweb/civil/.

Index

Abha (Gandhi's
    grandniece), 92
African Indians, 10, 40
    Boer War and, 41–42
    Green Pamphlet and, 37,
        39
    hail Gandhi, 29
    injustices against, 51, 53
        Black Act and, 47–50,
            52, 54
        British suppression
            and, 31–37
        Natal Indian Congress
            (NIC) and, 35–37, 39,
            42, 44
        nonviolence and, 44,
            49–51
        uniting of, 51–53
        victory of, 53–54
African National Congress,
    29, 33
Afrikaners, 31
Ahmadabad ashram, 55, 87
    hunger strike and, 59–60
Alfred Boy's High School,
    20
Ambedkar, Bhimrao Ramji,
    77
Amritsar massacre, 63–64
apartheid, 29, 33
archbishop of Canterbury, 92
Arjuna (Hindu hero), 24–25
Arnold, Edwin, 24
Ashe, Geoffrey, 41
ashram (communal
    settlement)
    Ahmadabad, 55, 59–60,
        87
    salt march and, 71
    Sevagram, 79

Asiatic Registration Law, 47
Assam (Indian province), 83
Atlantic Monthly (magazine),
    15
Attlee, Clement, 84

Ba (Kasturbai Gandhi), 21
Balasundaram, 36
Balfour (South African city),
    52
Baluchistan (Indian
    province), 83
Bean, Susan, 64
Beatles (band), 91
Benares Hindu University,
    57
Bengal (Indian province),
    83–84, 86
Besant, Annie, 57
Bhagavad Gita (Hindu epic
    poem), 24–25, 92
    Sermon on the Mount
        and, 26
Bharatiya Janata Party, 91
Bihar, 84
Birla, G. D., 59
Black Act, 47–48, 52, 54
    satyagraha and, 49–50
Boers (Dutch Africans), 31,
    35
Boer War, 41, 44
Bombay (Indian city), 28, 38
    salt march and, 72
    violence in, 84
Book of Matthew (Bible
    book), 26
Botha, Louis, 51
Brahman caste, 17
Brink, Andre, 29
British, 10

brief alliance of, 41–42
    Christianity and, 14–15
Gandhi and,
    goodwill mission of,
        75–77
    hunger strikes of,
        59–60, 66, 68, 77–78,
        90
    legacy of, 94
India's independence and,
    14–17, 60–63, 70, 82
    British deal and, 74–75
    government violence
        and, 72–74, 84
    negotiation of, 83–84
    Nehru and, 78–80,
        84–86
    partitioning and,
        83–84, 87–90
    salt march and, 71–72
    satyagraha success
        and, 72–73
    World War II and,
        78–81
Natal Indian Congress
    (NIC) and, 35–37, 39,
    42, 44
nonviolence and, 13, 44,
    49–51
Round Table Conference
    and, 75
schools of, 19
South Africa and, 10, 40
    Black Act and, 47–50,
        52, 54
    Boer War and, 41–42
    British suppression
        and, 31–37
    Green Pamphlet and, 37,
        39

injustice and, 31–37,
  51–54
uniting of, 51–53
victory of, 53–54
World War I and, 58
see also Gandhi, Mohandas
  Karamchand
British Labor Party, 84
Brown, Judith, 80
bubonic plague, 37–38
Buddha (Indian god), 60

Calcutta (Indian city), 42, 86
Cape Colony, 31, 35
  Union of South Africa
    and, 51
caste system, 17, 23, 28
  ashrams and, 55–56
  conditions of poor and,
    42–43
  Gandhi and, 35, 94
  political parties and, 77
  South Africa and, 31, 32
  untouchables and, 77–78
Catholics, 43, 92
celibacy (*brahmacharya*),
  45–47, 60
Champaran (Indian
  district), 58
Chaturmas (religious fast),
  18
Chauri Chaura (Indian
  town), 65–66
Chiang Kai-shek, 93
Christians, 43, 79, 90, 95
  British and, 14–15
  Hinduism and, 18
  Indian Cabinet and, 84
  NIC and, 35
  Sermon on the Mount
    and, 26
Christian Science Monitor
  (newspaper), 87
Churchill, Winston, 74–75, 81

"Civil Disobedience"
  (Thoreau), 10, 12
Civil Resistance, 10–11
  Kasturbai and, 21
  results of, 13
  suffering and, 12
cloth (*khadi*), 64
communal settlement. *See*
  ashram
conscience, 12–13
coolies (prejudiced term
  for Indians), 51
Courland (ship), 39–40
Cripps, Stafford, 79–81

Daily News (newspaper),
  23
Daily Telegraph (newspaper),
  23
Dalai Lama, 92
Delhi (Indian city), 63, 89
Dharsana Salt Works, 72–74
Direct Action Day, 84
Durban (South African
  city), 31, 33, 39–40, 53
  Phoenix Farm and, 45
Dutch, 31–33
  Indians' rights and, 35–37
  social reform and, 34–35
Dutch Africans, 31
Dyer, Reginald, 63

Economist (magazine), 91
Einstein, Albert, 92–93
Emancipation
  Proclamation, 95
Emergency Powers
  Ordinance, 76
*Essays, Speeches, Addresses,
  and Writings*
  (Naoroji), 26

Fischer, Louis, 59
Forester, E. M., 91

Freedom of Pietermaritzburg
  Medal, 33

Gandhi, Devadas (son),
  56
Gandhi, Harilal (son), 21,
  23, 30, 56
Gandhi, Karamchand
  (father), 14
  British rule and, 16–17
  caste and, 17
  death of, 21
  reaction to stealing, 20
Gandhi, Kasturbai (wife),
  20, 23
  ashram and, 56
  called to Gandhi's
    bedside, 77
  death of, 82–83
  goes to South Africa, 39
  passive resistance and,
    21, 30
  protests and, 52
Gandhi, Laxmidas (brother),
  19
Gandhi, Manilal (son), 30,
  56, 72
Gandhi, Mohandas
  Karamchand
  ambulance corps and, 42,
    45
  ashram project and, 55–56
  background of
    caste and, 17
    living in England and,
      22–24
    nanny and, 17
    parents, 14–18, 21, 28
    rediscovers Hinduism,
      24, 26–27
    religious faith and,
      17–18
    school and, 18–20,
      21–23, 26–27

vegetarianism and, 18, 20, 23–24, 26
bedside negotiations and, 77–78
Black Act and, 47–50, 52, 54
Boer War and, 41–42
burden of leadership and, 64–68
death of, 90–93
defies Western dress, 64
faith and, 37, 43, 78
Hindu-Muslim violence and, 43, 83–92
home rule and, 60–63
hunger strikes and, 59–60, 66, 68, 77–78, 82, 90
idealism of, 44–45
important dates of, 8–9
INC and, 42, 64–68
Independence Pledge and, 70
jail and, 49–52, 72, 74, 76, 82–83
as lawyer, 37
    brother's debts and, 29
    court debut, 28
    Indian law and, 28
    Johannesburg and, 44
    in South Africa, 31–37
    trouble with Ollivant and, 30
legacy of, 94–95
as Mahatma, 14, 56–57, 60, 82, 87
as mankind's conscience, 13
new resolution of, 68–69
NIC and, 35–37, 39, 42, 44
nonviolence and, 10
    anger lapse and, 57–58
    Chauri Chaura violence and, 65–66

Dharsana Salt Works and, 72–73
hartal violence and, 63–64
Hindu-Muslim conflict and, 85–86
Irwin-Gandhi pact and, 74–75
offensive measures and, 58–60
return to South Africa and, 40
salt march and, 71–72
satyagraha and, 10–11, 48–49
South African protests and, 48–54
suffering and, 11–13
partitioning and, 84, 88
personality of
    anger lapse of, 57–58
    helps poor, 42–43, 55, 58–60, 79
    humility of, 60, 78
    mob violence and, 40
    shyness and, 19–20, 28, 34
receives War Medal, 42
removed from train, 33
returns to India, 37–39
simple dress of, 55–56
spinning wheel and, 64, 68, 71, 91
troubled homecoming of, 30
World War I and, 58–60
Zulu rebellion and, 45–47
"Gandhi: Patron Saint of the Industrialist" (Renold), 59
Gandhi, Putlibai (mother), 14
death of, 28
Mohandas's travel to England and, 22–23

religious faith of, 17–18
Gandhi, Rramdas (son), 56
Germany, 58, 79
Godse, Nathuram, 92
Gokhale, Gopal Krishna, 42, 55
Green Pamphlet (Gandhi), 37, 39–40
Gromyko, Andrey, 92
Gujarati (Indian language), 10, 18–19, 33

Habib, Sheth Haji, 47
"Hang Old Gandhi on the Sour Apple Tree" (song), 40
Hardinge, Charles, 57
Hindus, 14, 79
    Bhagavad Gita and, 24–26
    beliefs of, 18
    charity and, 17
    marriage and, 20
    vs. Muslims, 43, 83–92
    NIC and, 35
    pacifism and, 24
    political parties and, 76, 77
    untouchables and, 77–78
Hoare, Samuel, 75

indentured servants, 35–36
    Boer War and, 42
    strikes and, 52–53
    women's arrests and, 52
Independence Pledge, 70
India
    Britain and, 14–17, 26, 60–63
    Gandhi's legacy and, 94
    independence of, 70, 82
        bedside negotiations and, 77–78
        British deal and, 74–75
        goodwill mission and, 75–77

negotiation of, 83–84
Nehru and, 78–80,
  84–86
partitioning and,
  83–84, 87–90
salt march and, 71–72
satyagraha success
  and, 72–73
World War II and,
  78–81
injustices of, 10
purification and, 68–69
Indian Cabinet, 84–85
Indian Home Rule (Hind
  Swaraj) (Gandhi), 61
Indian National Congress
  (INC), 42, 69
Amritsar Massacre and, 64
declared illegal, 76
Gandhi's leadership of,
  64–68
jail and, 65, 74, 76
Nehru and, 79
noncooperation and,
  69–70
partitioning and, 88
Quit India resolution and,
  82
Round Table Conference
  and, 75
salt march and, 72
Indian Opinion
  (newspaper), 44–45
Indians, 10
Asiatic Registration Law
  and, 47
Boer War and, 41–42
brief British alliance and,
  41–42
prejudice in South Africa
  and, 31–37, 40–54
women's voice and, 52
Irwin-Gandhi pact, 74–75
Irwin, Lord, 70, 74
Itihaas, 37

Jesus Christ, 26, 79, 95
Jinnah, Mohammed Ali,
  83–84, 88
Johannesburg, 44
  certificate burning and, 50

King, Martin Luther, Jr.,
  94–95
King George V, 57, 92
Krishna (Hindu god), 24, 60
Kshatriya caste, 17

Linlithgow, Lord, 82
London, 23–24, 27, 75
London Vegetarian Society,
  24

MacArthur, Douglas, 92
MacDonald, Ramsay, 74
Mahatma (Great Soul), 14,
  56–57, 60, 82, 87
  see also Gandhi, Mohandas
    Karamchand
Manchester Guardian
  (newspaper), 73
Mandela, Nelson, 33
Manu (Gandhi's
  grandniece), 92
Marquand, Robert, 87
Marshall, George C., 13
Methodists, 43
Mexican-American War, 10
Modi, Amrut, 87
Montague, Edwin, 62–63
Mountbatten, Lady, 88
Mountbatten, Lord, 88
Muslims, 14, 20, 79
  vs. Hindus, 43, 83–92
  Indian Cabinet and, 84–85
  NIC and, 35
  political parties and, 76–77

Naderi, SS (ship), 39–40
Naidu, Sarojini, 72

Naorohi, Dadabhai, 26
Natal (South African
  colony), 30, 35, 40
  parliament and, 39
  Phoenix Farm and, 45
  Union of South Africa
    and, 51
Natal Advertiser
  (newspaper), 40
Natal Indian Congress
  (NIC), 35–37, 39, 42, 44
Nazar, Mansukhlal, 44
Nehru, Jawaharlal, 78–80, 91
  Gandhi's death and, 93
  as prime minister, 84–86
New Testament, 26
noncooperation, 69–70
nonviolence (*ahimsa*), 10, 37,
  Black Act and, 49–50
  Champaran problem
    and, 58–59
  defying law and, 49–51
  Dharasna Salt Works
    and, 72–74
  Gandhi's legacy and, 94,
    95
  opponents' difficulties
    and, 54
  Quit India resolution
    and, 82
  satyagraha and, 48–49
  suffering and, 11–13
  Zulu rebellion and, 45
North-West Frontier
  (Indian province), 83

Ollivant, Charles, 30
Orange Free State, 31, 35
  Union of South Africa
    and, 51
Ottoman Empire, 58

Pakistan
  Gandhi's death and,

91–92, 94
  negotiating independence
    and, 83–84
  partitioning and, 88–90
Pall Mall Gazette
  (newspaper), 23
Parsi (religion), 84
passive resistance, 11, 48
Phoenix Farm, 45, 55
Porbandar (Indian city), 14,
  30
Pretoria (South African
  city), 33–35
prime minister (*diwan*), 14, 17
Punjab (Indian province),
  83–84
purification, 68–69

Quakers, 43
Queens College, 95
Quit India resolution, 82

Rajkot (Indian city), 14, 17,
  21, 28
Rambha (Gandhi's nanny),
  17
religion, 14–15, 17–18, 79
  Christians, 14–15, 18, 26,
    35, 43, 79, 90, 95
  Gandhi's speech and, 35
  Hindus vs. Muslims, 43,
    83–92
Renold, Leah, 59
Round Table Conference, 75
Rowlatt Acts, 63

Sabarmati Ashram, 56, 71
salt law, 70
salt march, 71–74
satyagraha (force of truth
  and love), 10
  Black Act and, 49–50

Champaran problem
  and, 58–59
Dharsana Salt Works
  and, 72–73
invention of, 48–49
opponent's difficulties
  and, 54
suffering and, 11
Selected Writings (Gandhi),
  48
Sermon on the Mount, 26
Seth, Dada Abdullah, 32
Sevagram Ashram, 79
Sheik Mehtab, 20
Shelley, Percy Bysshe, 24
Shukla, Rajukumar, 58
Sikhs (religion), 84, 90
Sind (Indian province), 83
Smuts, Jan Christian,
  49–51, 54
South Africa, 10, 40
  Boer War and, 41–42
  Green Pamphlet and, 37,
    39
  hails Gandhi, 29
  injustices against, 51, 53
    Black Act and, 47–50,
      52, 54
    British suppression
      and, 31–37
  Natal Indian Congress
    (NIC) and, 35–37, 39,
    42, 44
  nonviolence and, 44,
    49–51
  uniting of, 51–53
  victory of, 53–54
Story of Gandhi, The
  (Zinkin), 67
Sudra caste, 17
Supreme Court of South
  Africa, 51–52
suttee (funeral burning), 36

Tagore, Rabindranath,
  56–57, 73, 87
Thoreau, Henry David, 10, 24
  influence on Gandhi, 12
Tolstoy, Leo, 24, 43
Toynbee, Arnold, 91
Transvaal (Dutch colony),
  31, 33, 35, 44
  arrests and, 51–52
  Boer War and, 41
  satyagraha and, 49–50
  Union of South Africa
    and, 51
Trappist monks, 43
Truman, Harry, 92
Turkish, 58

Union of South Africa, 51
United Kingdom. *See*
  British
untouchables caste
  (harijans), 17, 38
  conditions of, 42–43
  Gandhi's hunger strike
    for, 77–78
  Indian Cabinet and, 84
  political parties and,
    76–77

Vaisya (merchant caste),
  17
Vishnu (Hindu god), 24–25
Vital Speeches of the Day
  (magazine), 95

West, Albert, 44
Willingdon, Lord, 76
Wireman, Billy O., 95
work stoppage (*hartal*), 63
World War I, 58, 60
World War II, 78–81, 83

Zinkin, Taya, 67

Picture Credits

Cover Photo: © Corbis/Hulton-Deutsch Collection

AP/World Wide Photos, 19, 22, 67, 93

Archive Photos, 15, 65, 73

Associated Press Radiophoto, 90

© Bettmann/Corbis, 12, 41, 56, 74

Brown Brothers, 75, 83, 89

© Corbis, 46

Culver Pictures, 31, 66

FPG International, 32, 79, 86

© Hulton-Deutsch Collection/Corbis, 11, 50, 57, 61, 71, 76, 88, 95

© Charles & Josette Lenars/Corbis, 25

Photofest/Icon Archives, 34

Popperfoto/Archive Photos, 23, 85

Stock Montage, 38, 51

© Underwood & Underwood/Corbis, 62

About the Authors

For the past twenty years, Mary Rodd Furbee has worked as a writer, editor, and television producer. She now teaches half time at the West Virginia University School of Journalism and writes nonfiction books for children and adults. Her work has appeared in the *Washington Post, Stars & Stripes, Cleveland Plain Dealer, Charleston Gazette, The Progressive, Goldenseal, Now and Then*, and other publications. Her books include *The Complete Guide to West Virginia Inns, Women of the American Revolution*, and *Outrageous Women of Colonial America*.

Mike Furbee is a research coordinator at the Center for Rural Emergency Medicine in Morgantown, West Virginia. His articles have been published in the *Annals of Emergency Medicine, Journal of Applied Sociology, Geo Info Systems*, and other magazines.